Young coöperators camping on the grounds of
the Crystal Palace, London

The ENGLISH COÖPERATIVES

By SYDNEY R. ELLIOTT

New Haven · Yale University Press

1937

Acknowledgments

The writing of any book describing how British consumers, through coöperation, have created the world's biggest Big Business is itself a coöperative enterprise. While responsibility for the factual accuracy of the present book and the arguments it advances is mine alone, I have received generous aid from many coöperative officers and organizations, and from my friends Mr. W. P. Watkins and Mr. John Thompson.

S. R. E.

February, 1937.

Contents

Illustrations

The English Coöperatives

I.

Introductory

EARLY in 1931 Great Britain was startled by the discovery of the consumer. World prices were collapsing. Stock values were crashing. Unemployment was rising steadily, relentlessly, to the new peak figure of three millions. Wages were cut. Expenditure on public works was replaced by subsidies to private enterprise. In a desperate effort to sustain price and profit levels, the nation slipped its Free Trade moorings and plunged into Protection.

At this moment of national strain, politicians and businessmen were surprised to observe that the Coöperative Movement created, capitalized and controlled by consumers was riding the storm triumphantly; that although private trading had reached another periodical dead end, the consumer in commerce had found the secret of perpetual progress, and had become the world's biggest Big Business.

Side by side with the great departmental emporiums, chain stores and small shops, there stood twelve thousand coöperative shops, the only shops in the country owned by their customers. Behind these coöperative stores, supplying them direct, were three hundred warehouses and productive factories. Supporting them were a bank, an insurance society and a national newspaper. Over their counters passed two shillings ten pence of every pound the public spent on food. They constituted the most important distributive agency in the nation's tea trade. They milled one third of the total flour imports, and baked one in every five loaves of Britain's bread. They purchased from farmers, processed and delivered one in every seven gallons of milk. Their coal depots stoked one in every seven domestic fires. They handled one tenth of the nation's meat supply. They were the biggest single unit in Empire trade. During a period when retail prices fell 10 per cent, their retail trade fell by only 4.33 per cent. While wholesale prices in the goods they handled fell 15 per cent, their whole-sale trade declined by less than 5 per cent. Although an es-sential part of the economic system—the Coöperative Move-ment, indeed, provides the most lucrative, most stable market for many of the products of private business—they were dis-tinguished from that system in two particulars. They were comparatively free from the restrictions placed upon planned development by the alternating booms and slumps which characterize Capitalism; and the profit deriving from their world-wide activities was returned to the consumer as divi-dend on his purchases, providing a mighty stimulant to the consumers' market upon which coöperative business grows and grows.

Credit for the discovery of the consumer goes to Lord Beaverbrook, former Canadian concrete trust builder, ex-Cabinet Minister, and now a newspaper owner, the William Randolph Hearst of Great Britain, aspiring to the political role of Warwick the king-maker. In search of a policy, his lordship had raided the elder Roosevelt's political wardrobe, donning the jacket and discarding the pants. He proclaimed his determination to protect "the little man" but not to "bust the trusts"; and the organized consumer, avowed enemy of the latter, was presented as a menace to the former. While it was small and weak, consumers' organization could be tol-erated. Now, however, it boasted the strength of a giant. It was in possession of too many sectors of trade in which the holy writ of orthodox economic law was not allowed to run.

The moment for attack on coöperators was propitious. Be-sides driving the country into Protection, the collapse in prices converted every store, every warehouse, every factory and many newspapers into bargain basements and dispensa-ries of free gifts. The effort to unload stocks declining in value sent distributive costs soaring. Rebates were everywhere on offer, percolating, ultimately and miraculously, to the final consumer. Great business houses dumped cutlery, clothing and furniture upon the purchasers of cigarettes, chocolates and meat extracts. Newspapers, fighting for the circulations which would sustain their revenues by giving them a claim to provide the best shopwindow for nationally advertized commodities, almost literally wrapped up silk stockings, pen knives and the works of Dickens in their news sheets, at a peak cost to their shareholders of £3,000,000 in 1933.

As a result of the fierce competition precipitated by manufacturers in fields outside their own, the economic confusion of the times became worse confounded. Before long there was a line-up in Parliament of the free gift dispensers and their trade opponents. A Parliamentary bill to end the practice of distributing gift coupons with goods was promoted. Introduced without the knowledge of the electorate, this bill occupied many hours of legislative time, then disappeared, mysteriously and without the consent of the public, when its chief protagonists, the big tobacco combines, settled their differences behind the scenes.

Attack on coöperators took many forms: that they did not pay income tax; that their dividend was a paltry inducement and a result of overcharging; that dividend was a form of price cutting and so great a menace to private enterprise that Parliament should enact its abolition; and so on. The Coöperative Movement swallowed every fresh wave of propaganda gas as though it were oxygen. Great Britain had discovered the consumer. It exploited the situation to insure that the consumer discovered himself. It trumpeted abroad the magnitude of its trade, the security of its capital, the power and promise of associated consumer effort. The facts made an impressive story.

The Coöperative Movement's six and a half million members embraced 14.58 per cent of the total population and

21.82 per cent of the population between sixteen and sixty-four years of age.[1] Their birth rate was high. Whereas in the ten years since 1921 the general population had increased by 4.7 per cent, the coöperative population had increased by 45 per cent.

In the ten years until 1935, sales of the retail societies had aggregated £2,245,000,000. On these sales there had been realized surpluses exceeding £200,000,000, every penny of which had been devoted to the enrichment of the individual coöperator. Through the retail societies, consumer-members controlled national wholesale and productive federations with an annual trade of £100,000,000. Coöperators were second only to the State as large-scale employers of labor. The number of their servants—300,000—had grown steadily through the 1924–29 period of rationalization, through the mild boom of 1929 and bitter slump of 1931. The organized consumer, too, was owner of £160,000,000 of capital in his retail societies, much of it accumulated dividend on purchases, all of it earning fixed rates of interest. Although Coöperation was front-page news, this volume of capital investment found no place in the financial columns of the Press. It was not listed on the Stock Exchange. It was not subject to the fluctuations of the money market.

Wherever he looked, the consumer saw the principle of mutuality in vigorous, vitalizing practice. In villages and cities, the opening of small shops and large emporiums was changing the nation's sky-line and testifying to the growth of Coöperation. In storm-tossed Eigg, whose Hebridean history told of conflict between Pict and Norseman, starvation was widespread as recently as 1918. The local authorities and the Government were unable to solve the problem of conveying food from the mainland at reasonable prices. Then fifty-seven crofters formed a coöperative society and found mutuality a solvent of their difficulties. Food supplies became

1. 1931 Census figures.

secure. Prices fell by one half, yet yielded a dividend of two shillings three pence in the pound. Crofters' savings, once hoarded in stockings and chimney corners, were earning 5 per cent. Private enterprise had almost deserted Jarrow, center of England's most depressed area, where the percentage of unemployed stood at 71.5, and, with the neighboring town of Hebburn-on-Tyne, averaged 50.8. Yet even here the local coöperative society had discovered the secret of economic stability. In the years 1931–34, sales fell from £449,329 to £397,592, but a dividend of 2s. 6d. had been maintained (representing an addition to the local community's purchasing power of nearly £50,000 every year), and reserve funds, that store of collective, noninterest-bearing capital which is the real financial basis of coöperative business in times of stress, had increased from £71,500 to £74,000. In the capital city, almost untouched by the Great Depression, the London Coöperative Society's membership was rocketing toward the six hundred and fifty thousand mark, and annual sales were in excess of £12,000,000. All over the country coöperators had similar tales to tell of how democracy in business was blunting the sharp edge of poverty's sword and diffusing new wealth and new hope among the people.

It is this story of the organized consumer in town and village, his history, his impact upon capitalist Britain, and the part he may play in a changing economic system, that the following pages will endeavor to unfold.

II.

Modern England in the Making

THE England of the early nineteenth century, which called forth the spirit and cradled the idea of Co-operation was, paradoxically, a land torn by conflict. Great social classes were disintegrating. Historic institutions were in decay. Swift, dramatic change marked developments in industrial technique. New theories of politics and ethics were being formulated to explain and excuse economic upheaval and social unrest. Paternal government, almost at the last gasp of its long life, was swaying between benevolence and repression. England's homogeneity found expression only in the traditional respect, shared by rich and poor alike, for essential human rights embodied in the law; and even that tradition, flouted by a new industrial bourgeoisie, was strained almost to the breaking point in the clash of classes. England was in the throes of Industrial Revolution.

Through eight hundred years feudalism and the overlordship of landowning barons had been sustained by a stable, if slowly changing, agricultural economy; an economy of which an essential feature was the cottager's right to graze his cattle on the village common and to cultivate his own patch on the manorial field. Feudalism forced serfdom and slavery on the people, but it gave them status; status strengthened by vigorous efforts, initiated in the reign of Edward I, to create a powerful central government with well-defined political ideas and fiscal methods. During the long twilight of feudalism English monarchs, having perceived how easily taxes could be raised from monopolies at home, encouraged the piracy of men like Francis Drake and Walter Raleigh in order to open up monopoly markets for English wool abroad; and the impact of desire for overseas expansion on domestic economy was turning England from a multiplicity of small holdings into a land of extensive sheep walks. Yet the poor man continued to enjoy status. For him the evils of divorce from the land, hastened by his own agitation against serfdom as well as by the changing structure of society, were mitigated by his ownership of the tools and raw materials of small-scale production. He carried on production in his own cottage. He wove the yarn his wife and children spun, and sold it in the only available market, the home market. He did not fear the competition of his fellows who also worked in rural homes. He could still milk his own cow, kill and cure his own meat, and grow his own vegetables. He heard but faintly the first reverberations of that fierce battle for wealth which the sudden expansion of trade was to precipitate.

Not until the second half of the eighteenth century did the face of England change finally and completely. The climax of an inclosure movement transferred millions of acres of common land from the people to the aristocracy by the simple act of promoting Parliamentary bills which the yeomen were too poor and too dispersed to oppose successfully. Farming was as popular a subject of discussion as His Majesty's mistresses and "the alienation of His Majesty's rational faculty" at the court of George III. Between 1760 and 1775, eight hundred and five acts of inclosure—nearly four times as many as had been passed in the reigns of Anne and the first two Georges—were approved. In all, it is estimated, four thousand private acts inclosed seven million acres during the century, the banditry which destroyed the small holder being legalized by a general Inclosure Act in 1801.

Meanwhile, in his humble home at Greenock an engineer, James Watt, was learning how to harness steam to machinery and liberate hitherto undreamed of sources of power. Watt effected the marriage of steam and machinery in 1764. Richard Arkwright, a Lancashire barber, who induced "men of property to engage with him to a large amount" of capital, adapted the ideas of earlier but less lucky inventors and pro-

duced a series of machines, all designed for steam, for card-
ing and roving cotton. Refinement followed improvement
until, in 1801, Dr. Cartwright, a Kentish clergyman, per-
fected a power loom capable of competing with the hand
weaver. An American agricultural factor decided that these
fateful inventions should be applied to cotton and not to wool,
England's staple export. Cotton, a Southern vegetable product, was cheap. Wool, a Northern animal product, was dear.
Whereas in 1795 imports of raw cotton were 18,000,000 lbs.;
in 1800, just prior to the coming of the power loom, they
were 56,000,000 lbs.; and in 1835, 333,000,000 lbs. Long
before the new machines were adapted for flax and linen and
wool, the factory dominated the once tranquil English scene.

The demand for steam stimulated the exploitation of England's coal resources and expanded the market for England's
steel. Men from the Weald of Sussex, where iron was smelted
with charcoal from the English oak, were transferred to
the new Black Country of the North and Midlands where
rich seams of ore could be mined and smelted with coal; and
the art that produced the iron gates and ornamental fire-
irons of quieter times was turned to the making of girders
and cranks and pistons and, later, to the manufacture of rails
for locomotives and plates for ships.

Between 1818 and 1829 one thousand miles of roads, all
sixty feet wide, were constructed of the graded hard stone
embedded in sand and earth which made famous the name of
McAdam, then Surveyor General of Roads. Where, before
1755, there were almost no canals, England in 1845 boasted
two thousand three hundred miles of canals and one thousand eight hundred miles of navigable river. Roads speeded
the romantic stage coach carrying mails and travelers. Canals
made possible the transport, however leisurely, of coal and
iron. Tom Paine, English king-breaker and American Con-
stitution-maker, designed in 1788 the first of the iron bridges
over which, within two decades, steam-driven iron trains were
to run. Steam, having revolutionized the home market, revo-

lutionized also travel by sea, making possible the capture of foreign markets unprotected against the flood of cheap English manufactures.

The home market was situated no longer in the quiet villages and small towns of rural England. Trade followed the road-maker, the canal-cutter, the bridge-builder and the rail-layer to the north, where water power to drive the mills flowed from the picturesque Pennines. There the grey swamps of Lancashire and the green fields of Yorkshire became the sites of great towns, seething whirlpools of steam and smoke and enterprise, all under the control of a new class of individual capital owners. Thus the workman, uprooted from his native soil, separated from ownership of his tools, and deprived of control over raw materials, lost both status and property. On the roads he was a vagrant; off them he was a trespasser. He had escaped the yoke of servitude to a landlord and acquired the badge of wage slavery. The Industrial Revolution had created neither the proletariat nor capitalist organization. It completed their evolution.

Contrary to modern experience, the death knell of economic systems a century ago was heard not in the groans of empty stomachs but in the hiccoughs of overfull bellies. Feudalism collapsed finally under the weight of new wealth and opportunity deriving from England's favored position as pioneer among manufacturing nations and among Empire trade builders. Once the granary of the world, Great Britain became, almost overnight, a food importer dependent for physical sustenance on the free exchange of goods for food. Almost inevitably, the growing numbers of laborers were the first casualties in the struggle waged by the rising industrialists against the established landlords—against that regulation both of trade and of the social position of labor called the Mercantile System, against restrictions upon the individual's right to do what he pleased with his own, and against the landlords' domination of Parliament. Herded into insanitary hovels in ill-planned towns, these laborers, their wives and children, worked long hours in ill-planned factories, to fill which even the pauper schools and lunatic asylums were emptied of their occupants. The poor food their paltry wages purchased was usually adulterated. For clothes they wore "suits of tatters, the getting on or off which is said to be a difficult operation transacted only in festivals and the high tides of the calendar." Drunkenness, illiteracy, vice and physical degeneration, every social evil of poverty, flourished in the new towns, making the condition of the people repugnant to all outside and to many within the circle of the newly rich.

Feudal government, frightened by the French Revolution of 1789 and aware of the horrors accompanying the depopulation of the countryside, but wilting under the pressure of industrial magnates, acted true to paternal type. It suppressed ruthlessly, in the Combination Acts of 1799–1800, every effort at trade union organization. As a measure of poor relief, it paid farmers subsidies in aid of wages but insisted that the poor man should obtain relief only in the parish in which he was born. Thus it rendered the poor man immobile and placed him at the mercy of fellow citizens who regarded his destitution as an additional burden upon local taxation. In defense of its landlord interests, the Government enacted in 1804 that home wheat must realize a price of 63s. per quarter before importation was allowed. In 1815 it passed the notorious Corn Laws raising the protected price to 80s. a quarter and slashing real wages severely. After the Napoleonic Wars, which established the colonial supremacy of England while increasing the National Debt from £247,000,-000 to £880,000,000, it abolished income tax, and increased indirect taxation falling most heavily on the poor. Whenever laborers congregated to protest against the machines which had robbed them of self-sufficiency or to denounce high prices now robbing them of their meager wages, as on the Fields of Peterloo, Manchester, in 1819, the soldiery were called out to massacre the mob. The rights of public meeting and of publication of opinion were suppressed. The right of search was given to magistrates. Every principle of law was trampled underfoot by autocratic authority.

Denied the opportunity of industrial organization, possessing no power over Parliament and deserted by the Church, whose practitioners professed to see a divine purpose in the social devastation wrought by man, the more independent laborers turned naturally to economic coöperation. As long ago as 1769 the weavers of Fenwick, Ayrshire, engaged in bulk buying, although how they distributed the small economies effected—the highest profit recorded in any single year was £4 1s.—is not known. In 1794 a village store was founded at Mongewell, Oxfordshire. All over the country local authorities were petitioned to establish flour mills to protect consumers against the jolly miller's practice of mixing china clay with flour. Several of these associations survived, but they lacked the cohesion of a national purpose and the appeal of a large idea.

On the other hand, the Industrial Revolution and all its works were being justified and buttressed by a growing body of economic and ethical doctrines. Thomas Malthus (1760–1834), for example, presumed to formulate his famous Law of Population in 1798, three years before the first census was taken, and long before any registration of births and deaths was attempted. A clergyman, Malthus challenged the current secular view that the potentialities of scientific production and the innate reasonableness of human beings would prevent population from outstripping the means of subsistence. He argued that sex would continue to be more reproductive of men than land would be of food and machines of goods. His theory reinforced strongly the opinion that working-class effort to raise wages was futile, since more bread in the larder would mean more mouths to fill at the table. Then, as now, desire was a strong digestive, whether of food or philosophy. The Law of Population gained much popularity in governing-class circles. In a cloud of witnesses to the ills caused the social body by spots on the sun and other strange, if divine, interventions, Adam Smith (1723–90), a Scottish Professor of Moral Philosophy, stood out as the great apologist of the new industrial order and the most deadly enemy of mercantilism. In simple, vivid language, he revealed the possibilities of division of labor. From the coöperation of men and machines, he pointed out, there flowed a saving of labor, of time, of cost, together with an increased productivity which was already tenfold and would become a hundredfold. This saving was the source of fresh capital which could be invested in machinery to promote further subdivision of labor. To carry coöperation into the distribution of the goods produced by industrial combination, however, would mean the destruction of individual incentive. Moreover, Smith accepted private, individual ownership of capital as blindly as Aristotle had accepted slavery. Coöperation to distribute wealth, therefore, implied collective action by the State, and it was fundamental to his creed that the best regulated State was one which made no regulation at all. In the remote event of a monopoly arising the State might interfere usefully. The more immediate danger that capital might become the monopoly of antisocial elements or incompetents was resolved by free competition. This same competition required the removal of restrictions on home trade and tariffs on foreign exchange. Finally freedom to compete and freedom of trade safeguarded the consumer and the wage earner. For the one there were low prices when production was plentiful. For the other there were high wages when labor was scarce. Pursuing their individual interests, men pursued also the greatest good of the greatest number; and thus—for Adam Smith, be it remembered, was a moral philosopher as well as an economist —"divine harmony" was achieved under a baton wielded by "the invisible hand" of an omniscient conductor. When these ideas became copybook maxims, it required only the concentration of capital through the introduction of paper currency and the beginning of joint-stock banking in 1826 to secure the fruits of the Industrial Revolution for private enterprise.

While there were sporadic and easily suppressed risings of the people against their conditions, the real challenge to laissez faire came from men of influence who put loyalty to English tradition before worship of material wealth. That tradition reached back to the days of Magna Charta when all men became subject to Common Law, and the free citizen was given the right of trial by his equals. When Edward I wrested from the barons their power to enforce taxes and gave the economic status quo expression in a political system, he gave birth to two ideas which have remained paramount in the governance of England ever since: the idea of State or group responsibility, whether much or little, for the welfare of the individual, and the twin idea of democracy. The political State might be subverted by this or that oligarchy, but it was capable of expansion and of change. As it triumphed over the claim of the Stuart kings to be regarded as rulers by divine right, it became more and more capable of change without physical revolution. Indeed, the very fact that, in the early years of the nineteenth century, an industrial oligarchy was subverting the State in a way oppressive of the people and offensive to the social conscience, brought idealists and reformers into sharp opposition with authority. They demanded extension of the franchise to the middle class and, in the Reform Bill of 1832, the vote was conceded to one in every six adults. They agitated for the abolition of rotten or pocket boroughs, whose Parliamentary representation had been a perquisite of the landowning class for centuries, and the same Reform Bill abolished these boroughs. They secured a revision of the Poor Law, adding little to the comfort of the poor since it made destitution the basis of relief and implied that the unemployed man was alone responsible for his poverty, but ending the corruption of the subsidy-in-aid-of-wages principle. They defended Labor's right to combine. Even more important, they insisted that businessmen should insure the efficient government of the new towns growing round their factories, and that care of the law and social services should be transferred from the country gentlemen and parsons, who were unpaid Justices of the Peace, to properly elected local authorities. In 1835 the Municipal Reform Act established local governing councils and gave expression to the administrative capacity of the citizen who, as the franchise extended, became every man and every woman. Here Collectivism first found life in municipal organization of the police, of sanitation and, later, of gas and water and transport. Here, too, was developed the committee system with its invaluable contribution to the difficult art of self-government, and the method of the grant-in-aid, from the central government through the local authority to those voluntary organizations promoting health and education which laid the foundation for the mighty structure of social services now covering the whole country. Artistic England might seek escape from the harsh realities of life by following Wordsworth and Southey to the Lakelands; but Blake condemned the "dark Satanic mills," Shelley thundered against "waste followed by lame famine, wealth by squalid want," Byron excoriated the landlords, and Lady Byron, deserted by her Don Juan, found solace in financing coöperative propaganda among working men. Discontent was widespread enough. Its need was for direction, and this was given it by Robert Owen.

A Welshman, born in 1771, Owen had gone from a poor home in Newtown, Montgomeryshire, to London as a draper's apprentice and, like many another ambitious lad of his generation, had been attracted by the possibilities of the fast growing cotton industry. At the age of twenty-nine he had acquired sufficient wealth and reputation to become managing director of the New Lanark Mills of David Dale, a benevolent Quaker, whose daughter he married. Owen's capacity for making money did not win his partners to his scheme for social reform, but, fortunately for the success of an experiment which was to make history, they did not interfere seriously with his control until 1828.

At New Lanark, Owen rehoused the work people, reduced

their hours of toil, and raised their wages. He abolished the truck system by which masters ran stores and held wages as security against the goods workers felt compelled to purchase. He substituted for truck shops coöperative stores, the profits of which built and financed the first infant school in Great Britain. In the London *Times* in 1834 he was able to write truthfully: "For twenty-nine years we did without the necessity for magistrates or lawyers; without a single legal punishment; without any known poor's rate, without intemperance or religious animosity. We reduced the hours of labour, well-educated all the children from infancy, greatly improved the condition of the adults . . . paid interest on capital, and cleared upward of £300,000 of profit."

On the anvil of business experience Owen hammered out a philosophy of life which, with terrific zeal for propaganda, he issued as a call to everyone in authority. Philanthropists and reformers were at variance with many of Owen's views. From the practical results of New Lanark and the proof it offered of the economy of high wages, however, they drew the inspiration which defeated the pessimism of Malthus and Adam Smith and forced Government to concede the case for factory legislation. An inoperative Act of 1802, designed to prevent apprentices in the cotton trade from being worked more than twelve hours a day, gave place to an 1819 Act forbidding the employment of children under nine and reducing adult working hours from sixteen to twelve. This Act depended for its effectiveness upon the common informer, and since he could only be a workman certain to be victimized if he informed against his master, it failed in its purpose. Yet it represented a beginning. It stimulated the agitation for a Ten-Hour Bill which secured, in 1833, the prohibition of night work in mills for all under twenty-one, and the appointment of factory inspectors.

Reform begets courage. Factory operatives themselves were beginning to listen to agitators, were forming "underground" trade unions. For them, too, Owen had a message.

The Father of Modern Socialism was no doctrinaire. He was as willing to sweep society clean with the broom of revolution as to reform its institutions. He had supported the 1824 campaign to secure the repeal of the Combination Acts and rescue trade unions from illegality. Now, in 1834, he launched a Grand Consolidated Trades Union which, by fixing the weekly subscription at 3*d*. and promising payments up to 10*s*. per week "during a strike or turn out," swept even the poorest among the laborers into his organization. Lodges of industrious females were linked to the Grand Consolidated which soon found itself with large powers but little purpose. The enterprise revealed more clearly Owen's disappointment at the paucity of political reform effected in 1832 than any sound plan for realizing the social revolution. The Grand Consolidated's failure to save six men of Dorset, the Tolpuddle Martyrs, from transportation on the charge that the trade union they had founded was a secret society— only one of many gross breaches of the legal code by a frightened magistracy—brought a grandiose effort to an ignominious end.

Owen's real hope was that, by some chimerical means, work people could engage during a strike in producing for themselves; and this idea, that workingmen could form productive communities and there solve the social problem, was the driving force of Owenism.

Owen did not attribute the success of the New Lanark Mills to his own business genius, but to the naïve moral aphorisms with which his Celtic mind clothed sound business policies. These aphorisms he glorified into principles of action. He conceived of a series of New Lanark experiments covering all land and all industry and, ultimately, rescuing all men from moral wrong and economic error. In every campaign he swayed between patronage and self-help. Patronage took the form of inducing rich men to build Communistic communities.

At Orbiston, near Motherwell, the aristocratic Archibald

James Hamilton, son of General Hamilton of Dalzell, joined Owen in promoting such a community. Young Hamilton had fought at Waterloo, but a honeymoon trip to Paris had aroused his Republican sympathies. As Lord Lieutenant of the County of Lanark he refused to mobilize the militia to suppress insurgent laborers in 1819. Now he joined Owen in inviting the wealthy to subscribe two thousand £50 shares to establish Communism on the family estate. There was to be a fixed rate of interest for shareholders. A reserve fund was to be accumulated out of which the tenants were to buy the land. No response was forthcoming until an Edinburgh Quaker, Abram Combe, put up £19,995, for two hundred and ninety-one acres of Hamilton's land and mortgaged it to finance the experiment which started in March, 1825. Combe was no Communist. He objected to the Owenite proposal that, whether its members contributed much or little to the success of the community, they should be paid according to their needs. So Orbiston started without Owen's support.

From the beginning the community was mismanaged. All sorts and conditions of men flocked to the little village and enjoyed its shelter, however useless their training or unsavory their character. Their rowdiness fed the suspicion of the surrounding countryside. Orbiston became known as Babylon. For a brief moment, success seemed to be within sight. Combe himself took charge and insisted on the three hundred residents working efficiently and observing strict rules of personal conduct. He attracted the assistance of Alexander Campbell, one of the most intelligent of Scottish revolutionary workingmen who later founded the Glasgow Trades Council and, in 1867, helped to force onto the Statute Book a Master and Servant Act which equalized before the law the contract between employer and employee. Campbell set up an iron foundry and organized a horticultural company. Weaving and spinning were introduced. Good management proved the economy of the coöperative way of life. Then came a battle of the doctrinaires. In September, 1826, Combe

fell ill, and the editorship of the community paper passed into the hands of an Owenite who demanded the full application of the Communist principle. Orbiston was divided into
two factions whose adherents would not sit at the same table.
On his deathbed Combe conceded the Owenite claims. Panic-
stricken bondholders raised their interest charges from three
and a half per cent to five per cent. Campbell pledged his own
credit in a desperate effort to save the community from debt
and was lodged in Hamilton Gaol. The whole scheme collapsed. Orbiston was the cemetery of both the wealth and the
heart of Archibald James Hamilton. He died in 1834, aged
forty.

Almost the same story can be told of the other communities—Ralahine, Ireland (1830–33); Queenwood, Norfolk
(1840–44); and New Harmony, Indiana (1825–27)—the
story of reformers with more faith than capital, and of failure to fuse fine individual endeavor into collective achievement.

Owen's schemes of self-help did not boast much greater
success. They were rooted in the coöperative store which
seemed even to him too humble an instrument to translate
men from a system wherein "production and consumption
are unnaturally restrained to the new moral world," and he
regarded their formation as a mere incident in his campaign.
Yet they possessed survival value. They taught workingmen
the real arts of combination and administration. They concentrated a multiplicity of tiny enterprises into a nationwide
movement. They won wide acceptance for the most fertile of
all of Owen's ideas, the idea of taking the profit element out
of price.

In 1821, London workingmen formed a Coöperative and
Economical Society in order to establish two hundred and
fifty families in a self-supporting community. The immediate
object was to buy goods at wholesale prices, sell them to
members at retail prices, and capitalize the difference in
prices on behalf of the larger project. An estimate of the di-

rect material benefit of community trading and living for the fortunate two hundred and fifty families makes interesting reading today. Rent at £10 per family cost £2,500 in the outside world; but to a community only £900—a clear saving of £1,600 per annum. On bread there was a saving of £531; on beer (sixty gallons daily) £900, and on meat £1,386. A communal expenditure of £13,000, it was anticipated, would yield a standard of living represented by individual family budgets totaling £20,000. To coöperative storekeeping was assigned the humble role of midwife at the birth of a better social order; and coöperative societies having "the grand ultimate object of . . . community on land" flourished under the name of Union Shops to the number of three hundred in 1830.

Their modest success spelt ruin. Members were unwilling to regard profits as indivisible. Whatever the distant ideals animating leaders, the rank and file desired immediate, tangible benefits. Housewives exercised their purchasing loyalty only in respect of commodities priced lower than at private shops. Since the societies enjoyed no legal protection, they were the prey of every petty crook. Moreover, after the collapse of the Grand National Consolidated Trades Union, capture of the State alone seemed to promise rapid results to rebellious workers. The enfranchised middle class, determined to destroy the Corn Laws and secure the cheap food which would insure cheap labor, was identifying itself with the people through the Anticorn League founded in 1836, financed by mill owners and supported by great popular figures like Richard Cobden (1804–65) and John Bright (1811–89). They pointed to high prices as the root cause of social unrest. They deplored the tentative nature of the approach to Free Trade, since of the one thousand five hundred commodities subject to tariff in 1824 only two hundred and fifty had been put on the free list. Out of this temporary Liberal-Labor alliance, there sprang the Chartist Movement. It whipped the workingmen of England into frenzied support for its six-point program: manhood franchise; vote by ballot; annual Parliaments; payment of M.P.'s; abolition of property qualifications for M.P.'s; and equal electoral districts.

As the People's Charter frightened the governing classes, so it aroused ever fiercer enthusiasm among the masses, and trade unions and coöperative stores were left to perish. In vain did Alexander Campbell implore workingmen to seek economic salvation before political emancipation. From the aging handloom weavers who, incapable of accommodating themselves to life in factories, still hankered after their old status, Chartism drew its most uncompromising recruits. For them it represented the proletarian revolution. Led by Feargus O'Connor, M.P. (1794–1855), soon to be confined in a lunatic asylum, the Movement swept from success to excess. With the repeal of the Corn Laws in 1846 the middle class withdrew their patronage. Two years later came the final throw. A demonstration was called on Kensington Common, London, to present a petition, said to have been signed by six million persons (the real figure was under two million). Parliament took the implied threat seriously. It passed a special bill making any attempt to overawe it illegal and recalled the eighty-year-old Duke of Wellington to defend Westminster. The civil police, however, were strong enough for all emergencies. They merely warned O'Connor not to cross the Thames. He tamely asked the crowd to disperse. The revolution was at an end.

Robert Owen died in 1858, friendless despite the impetus he had given to every one of the mighty movements of his time, and unaware of the appearance of a new generation destined to build him a monument in the world-wide Coöperative Movement. Of this generation were the Rochdale Pioneers, youthful, thirsting for the education offered them by voluntary agencies, and understanding the lessons of recent history. Their guide and mentor was Charles Howarth, aged thirty. His lieutenants were James Smithies, aged twenty-nine; William Cooper, aged twenty-two; and Samuel Ashworth, aged nineteen. These men, all associated with the cotton trade in one of the ugliest of Lancashire's ugly towns, were not intent on regaining lost status but upon winning a place of decency and dignity in society. As citizens they sought a contract with the State, they demanded the vote. As producers they determined to give labor, through organization, more equal bargaining power with the landlord, the capitalist and the entrepreneur. As consumers they desired to realize Owen's conception of "price without profit." The days of blind reliance upon demagogues were over. Practical, mutual aid, inspired by high social purposes, had made a real beginning.

III.

Onward from Rochdale

STORIES about the Rochdale Pioneers are legion. Many of them are apocryphal. Yet the facts of achievement speak louder and more romantically than the words of all the imaginative historians.

Their number, it is said, comprised twenty-eight weavers whose capital of £28 was raised in weekly subscriptions of a few coppers. Their first stock, housed in a humble shop at Toad Lane, consisted of flour, oatmeal, sugar, butter and candles. The bare shelves excited as much derision as the informal opening ceremony on December 21, 1844; for then the bold adventurers suffered so much from stage fright that it was left to a woman to pull down the shutters and reveal to the waiting crowd how poor was the material upon which the Pioneers had built large hopes. Fortunately, in their rules, their statement of objectives, and their method of trading, the young enthusiasts of Rochdale showed common sense well calculated to attract wide support.

The Rochdale Society of Equitable Pioneers was registered under the Friendly Societies Act on October 24, 1844. Included in its book of rules was this seven-point program:

(1) The objects of this Society are to form arrangements for the pecuniary benefit and improvement of the social and domestic condition of its members, by raising a sufficient amount of capital in shares of one pound each, to bring into operation the following plans and arrangements:

(2) The establishment of a store for the sale of provisions, clothing, etc.

(3) The building, purchasing, or erecting of a number of houses, in which those members desiring to assist each other in improving their domestic and social conditions may reside.

(4) To commence the manufacture of such articles as the Society may determine upon, for the employment of such members as may be without employment, or who may be suffering in consequence of repeated reduction in their wages.

(5) As a further benefit and security to the members of this Society, the Society shall purchase or rent an estate or estates of land, which shall be cultivated by the members who may be out of employment or whose labor may be badly remunerated.

(6) That, as soon as practicable, this Society shall proceed to arrange the powers of production, distribution, education and government, or in other words, to establish a self-supporting home colony of united interest, or assist other societies in establishing such colonies.

(7) That for the promotion of sobriety a Temperance Hotel be opened in one of the Society's houses as soon as convenient.

In truth, the Pioneers became absorbed at once in realizing the first two points of their program. Points three, four, five and six may have been a concession to Chartists and Owenites who could plead the hardship occasioned by a recent lockout of flannel weavers as a reason for revolutionary action. Point seven, it is recorded, was incorporated following a discussion held in a favorite beer house! The program served its purpose. It recognized the general interest of those it was designed to recruit. Like the Roman code of laws, it could be twisted and strained to accord with the ideas of reasonable men at any time.

More important, and rather less flexible, were the rules laid down by the Pioneers to guide their trade practices. Capital was to be raised by the Society's own members, to whom the benefactions of charitable individuals and State assistance in any form were abhorrent; and the capital so raised was to receive a fixed rate of interest, thus preventing service to capital transcending the basic idea of service to the consumer. The Society accepted a moral obligation to insure full weight and measure, and market prices were to be charged. Credit was neither to be asked nor given. Membership was open to all, whatever their political or religious views, and to men and women on equal terms. To sex equality was added an assurance of democratic government. Every member, however large or small his capital holding might be, was to have one vote in the election of the officers and committee who would manage the Society and render an account of their stewardship to a periodical meeting of members. A definite proportion of profits—2½ per cent—was to be allocated to educational purposes.

Besides these rules, which clearly made the general interest of the consumer paramount, the Pioneers determined to apply a new principle in coöperative trading which was to bring self-help within the capacity of the most downtrodden of the poor —the principle of dividend on purchases. When the surplus arising from trade had been charged with all the normal expenses of business, it was not to pass into the pockets of the members in their capacity as shareholders (they had already received a fixed rate of interest), but into the purses of the housewives in proportion to the volume of their purchases from their own store. Coöperators in Rochdale had discovered the secret of taking profit out of price. No longer were they to labor and wait for the benefits of a distant millennium. The rewards of purchasing loyalty were to be immediate and tangible: pure food, full weight, and, every six months, a dividend of a few shillings or a few pounds which they could convert into clothing or furniture, or allow to accumulate in the funds of the Society as personal capital.

The inner life of the Society, revealed in the early minute book, was tense with human drama. There were acute personal differences, the results of political disputes and ignorance of business. Throughout the three years of depressed trade, 1846–49, there were appeals from members in distress, responded to generously, and forced sales of shares, imposing heavy burdens on the Society's slender resources. Rochdale's

A group of the original Rochdale Pioneers

Where it all started. The first coöperative store,
opened at Toad Lane, Rochdale, in 1844

Pioneers, however, were possessed of high courage. They fostered the idea that the welfare of their association stood above
every personal interest, fostered it so sedulously that members gave gladly of their time to act as voluntary shop assistants. Slowly they proceeded to build up their stock of salable
articles and to employ full-time paid officers who (a shrewd
blow at nepotism, this) could not be members of the board
of management.

Given at last an efficient technique, coöperative storekeeping began to win a reputation in which the dreary record of
former failures was forgotten. George Jacob Holyoake
(1817–1906), fighter for freedom of religious opinion and
for a free Press, and John Stuart Mill (1806–73), most constructive of the Liberal economists, became the self-appointed
propagandists of Rochdale Coöperation. By 1851, one hundred and fifty societies were operating in Lancashire, Yorkshire and the industrial Midlands of Scotland.

Two economic factors made the moment of launching the
Rochdale venture propitious. There was a mass of social distress presenting a problem every section of the working-class
community was glad to mitigate. Following the trade crisis
of 1847, there was also an industrial boom in which prices
rose sharply, yielding profit margins sufficiently large to insure attractive dividends upon purchases. Sir Robert Peel's
budgets of 1842 and 1845, the abolition of the Corn Laws in
1846, and the final repeal, in 1849, of all restrictive legislation upon shipping simplified those tariffs they did not sweep
away, and made possible the completion of Free Trade by
Gladstone within the next decade. The Bank Charter Act of
1844 effected many financial reforms. From Australian and
Californian goldfields new nuggets of the money standard
were being mined to help inflate prices and roll back depression's cloud. India's vast market, followed by China's, fell
before the assaults of British enterprise. Wages began to rise
slowly, averaging 11s. 7d. a week in 1860 and improving
gradually thereafter. Capitalists opposed wage increases and

Trade Unionism as a matter of course. Compared with the big game now offered by the growing market, however, the small pickings afforded by the truck system were something they could scorn. Soon a ten-and-a-half-hour working day, with Saturday a half holiday, became universal. Trade unionists themselves, inspired by Rochdale Coöperation, began to seek the rewards of compromise and contract rather than the fruits of force, and found their rewards more lasting. Many of the important unions withdrew from their local branches power to declare strikes. The ably led Amalgamated Society of Engineers (now the Amalgamated Engineering Union), having federated several trade organizations, built up a voluntary system of sick benefit and superannuation allowances. In 1851, with 11,000 members, it was more powerful in size and annual income than any trade society in history. Seeking publicity for their activities, the engineers' leaders freed Trade Unionism from its old masonic mummery. They created for Labor a reserve fund which, during a six months' strike in 1852, bore a financial burden of £43,000, and they forged an instrument of collective bargaining which no capitalist employer could break or ignore. In their battle for recognition the trade unions rallied the general public to their side as never before. Charitable aristocrats donated large cheques to strike funds. A group of Christian Socialists gave generously of time and money to the campaign which secured the legal status of trade unions in 1871.

These Christian Socialists, typical of the best minds among the middle classes, were to wield enormous influence in awakening the spirit of Liberal reform in Great Britain. Frederick Denison Maurice (1805–72), Christian philosopher and "the greatest mind since Plato," was their leader. His fearless advocacy of the view that Christianity had an answer to the social problem rallied to his side men like John Malcolm Ludlow (1821–1911), who became Registrar of Friendly Societies; Charles Kingsley (1819–75), the rector of Eversley and author of *Alton Locke*; Tom Hughes (1822–96),

Liberal, a barrister and hero of every reader of *Tom Brown's
School Days*; and Edward Vansittart Neale (1810–92), a
barrister counting Cromwell among his forbears, who spent
his large personal fortune in the cause of Labor and was to
become the distinguished secretary of the Coöperative Union.
In a manner reminiscent of Voltaire, the Christian Socialists
scattered broadsheets among the workingmen of England
during Chartist times. "Many of you are wronged, and many
besides yourself know it," they told the people, but "you
want more than Acts of Parliament can give." This "something more," whether provided by Trade Unionism or Coöperation, had to be protected by Acts of Parliament. Besides
helping to make articulate the aspirations of the Rochdale
Pioneers, the Christian Socialists brought them much needed
legal advice. They formulated and forced through Parliament the Industrial and Provident Societies Act of 1852—
the first dim outline of a new commercial code—which gave
legal sanction to coöperative storekeeping. Ten years later
they secured the passage of addenda which enabled corporate
bodies to hold more than one acre of land and extended to co-
operative societies the privilege of limited liability—the limitation of the individual's responsibility for the debts incurred
by a company, of which he is a shareholder, to the amount of
his individual shareholding—and made possible the investment of capital by a single society in a federation of societies.
This "Coöperators' Charter" did not receive the royal as-
sent without considerable effort, including the arrival at
Westminster of a Lancashire deputation of enthusiasts intent
upon large coöperative development, their expenses being
met by the first coöperative political levy of ½d. per member. Moving the second reading,[1] Mr. J. H. Sotheron-

1. In the British House of Commons, the first reading of a bill is usually
introductory and informal. The second reading evokes whatever opposition the
bill arouses, and may result in its rejection. The third reading follows the review of the bill by a committee of members who may amend it in detail. The
bill, of course, is liable to defeat on its third reading.

Estcourt, a Conservative ex-Home Secretary, pleaded that the hundred and fifty coöperative societies, doing a trade of £1,500,000 per annum, were composed of men who, far from having embarked on a pleasure cruise, were "pulling for their lives in a mere skiff and deserved to be protected from the surging billows on every side." A further amendment of the Act, in 1867, ended the limitation of one coöperative society's investment in another and indicated the trend of coöperative development. From the simple act of buying goods for retail sale, coöperators were proceeding to buy goods in bulk for wholesale distribution. The societies created by individual consumers had become the controlling units of a federal society whose warehouses were soon to dominate many of the business centers of England and Wales.

By 1851, some form of coöperative wholesaling had become a necessity. Retail societies were competing against each other in wholesale markets. Their still puny individual strength was not a sufficient safeguard against irritating boycotts. In 1856 the Pioneers, whose ownership of a corn mill had added to their prestige, opened a wholesale department operating like any other wholesale house. Within three years the venture failed, showing a loss of £1,500. Undismayed, Abraham Greenwood (1824–1911), a pioneer Chartist and secularist, and acknowledged leader of the new Movement, sustained his propaganda for the formation of a wholesale society. At Jumbo Farm, almost equi-distant from Rochdale, Manchester, and Oldham, and rich in Owenite memories, Greenwood met his friends from neighboring societies and inspired them with his revelation that Coöperation was an economic theory as well as a day-to-day practice.

"There is the Rochdale Pioneer Society with its nine grocery branches all supplied and managed by the Central Store in Toad Lane," he told them. "The head shopman at each branch store makes out a list of requirements for his branch on a form provided for the purpose, and sends it to the central place of business; then the manager gives directions to the railway or canal company where the goods are lying to send such and such quantities of articles specified to such and such branch store named on the delivery order." So was developed the carefully measured, *known* market, ending haphazard organization of business and effecting economies which, through voluntary Coöperation, were returned to the consumer. Warming to this theory of the known market, then at variance with the teachings of the economists, Greenwood continued: "Now the central store stands in the same relation to its branches as an agency would be to the stores joining it . . . the time in goods through the agency will be a trifle longer and the transactions very much larger, but only requiring the same amount of labour to work the agency as it requires to work the Rochdale Store with its branches"; and he set out these conditions of success:

(1) An agency in Manchester or Liverpool doing business for ready money only.

(2) No profits but a small commission on the business done for each society to cover agency expenses, and nothing more.

(3) Business to be done only with coöperative establishments.

(4) Compulsory dealing with the agency by affiliated stores.

(5) Capital to be raised in proportion to society's membership.

(6) Each society to pay its own carriage charges.[2]

Curiously enough, although Greenwood had unfolded a plan which was to obviate the need for the new Society's incurring heavy financial obligation—yet another form of economy from which the coöperative consumer derived benefit—he failed to find what was to be the real solvent of the difficulties hampering coöperative development in the field of wholesale trade, the solvent of dividend on purchases. The

2. Redfern, *The Story of the C.W.S.*, p. 407 *et seq.*

North of England Wholesale and Industrial Provident Society, the result of Greenwood's advocacy, achieved but a moderate success. The committees of many societies preferred to purchase in the open market. Buyers "liked to give orders and bestow patronage."

By November, 1864, however, Rochdale principles had been applied to wholesale Coöperation. The Coöperative Wholesale Society, charging its constituents current prices and returning to them a dividend on purchases, had entered upon that period of expansion which was to make it the biggest unit in the world's biggest Big Business. In 1867, a Coöperative Insurance Society was established on the same Rochdale principle. One year later the Scottish C.W.S. began operations. Then came the opening of a C.W.S. branch at Newcastle, the creation of an *ad hoc* federation to launch the Coöperative Press, and the development of a banking department.

America's cotton famine had cast a shadow over Lancashire. The news organ of private grocers had tried to initiate a boycott of coöperative societies. Yet the decade from 1864, while it witnessed the growth of coöperative federations and the assembling of the framework of a Movement that had become truly national, was comparatively uneventful. Each morning the out-of-work Lancashire weaver, visiting the factory gates to learn whether America's Civil War had ended, was seized with fear that if the mill's furnaces went out they might never be relit, and intoned his historic prayer, "God keep our factory chimneys warm." Each evening at his trade union or coöperative society meeting, he passed resolutions in favor of the Abolitionists and voted guineas to the Cotton Famine Relief Fund. As for the boycotters of Coöperation, they could be ignored. The whole working-class movement was flourishing in the noontide of Liberalism. Believing that the future of Labor depended on winning legal recognition for working-class organization, and the opening of schools and Parliament to the people, coöperators and trade unionists were rejoicing in the extension of the franchise to town workers in 1867 (to be followed by general adult male suffrage in 1884, when the vote was given to rural workers), and in the free Education Act of 1870. By now the world had become one trade unit. Indeed, the world market had asserted its influence, even on England's remotest villages, when in 1857 the collapse of America's railway boom sent shocks through Great Britain, causing the suspension of those clauses in the Bank Act which tied currency issue to gold reserves. Again, in 1866, financial chaos followed the cotton crisis and England's gold standard made another journey "west." But between 1850 and 1870 coal output rose from fifty-six million tons to a hundred and ten million tons, shipbuilding more than doubled, and exports swelled in value from £71,000,-000 to £199,000,000. The grossest evils of the factory system had been eliminated by factory legislation, ever broadening in its scope. Britain's Red Ensign was fluttering over ships rendered by statute more seaworthy than before. Town sanitation, civic services and slums were coming under public review, and the more enterprising municipal authorities were contemplating collective ownership of gas works, water supplies, transport and other trading ventures.

Besides freeing trade, Sir Robert Peel (1788–1850), whose wealth came from Lancashire, had given a new turn to Tory policy. Calling for the conservation of the good and the purging of the bad in existing institutions, he had routed the reactionaries in his own party. The heritage he bequeathed had helped to make all England Liberal. Chartism was as dead as the Duke of Wellington. Imposing figures like Disraeli (1804–81), a Conservative in the Liberal tradition, and Gladstone (1809–98), an uncompromising Radical, filled the political stage. The Government was powerful abroad. Already the black man was carrying a large share of the white man's burden. Government could afford to be benevolent at home. Although the battles of the day were for freedom of opinion rather than for bread, the grant of the franchise to

Burke's "swinish multitude" had made the social problem the major issue in politics. Outside Scandinavia, no other people was to arrive at that pregnant moment without violent revolution. "The condition of the people" dominated Parliamentary debate. Collective regulation was "blocking the downward way" to anarchy. Their sober movements having won concessions that were safe if not spectacular, the leaders of the working class were content to let the fruits of association ripen slowly in the sun of education and political democracy.

Coöperators were in tune with this mood. Their idealism found expression in the launching of cultural classes, forerunners of a nation-wide adult education movement, and in providing the country with its first free libraries, this multiplicity of educational effort being financed out of the surpluses of their growing trade. They were discovering, too, a need for discussing their policy in relation to the outside world in an atmosphere somewhat freer than that of the retail or wholesale business meetings, where questions of business detail took priority. So there arose in 1869, under the inspiration of the Christian Socialists, a Central Board which linked up numerous district committees and created the modern Coöperative Union. As the ethical watchdog of Coöperation, the Coöperative Union fostered and coördinated all nontrading activities of coöperators, giving them purposive direction and, through an annual Coöperative Congress, an authentic voice. When the Union became conterminous with the entire trading movement, including retail societies and wholesale federations in its membership, as it did in the Seventies, Coöperation was well equipped for the giant tasks of consolidation and expansion to which it set its hand.

John Thomas Whitehead Mitchell (1828–95) had succeeded to the chairmanship of the C.W.S., bringing to that still youthful organization rare qualities of constructive leadership. A fatherless child, Mitchell had been brought up in a Rochdale beerhouse by a mother whom he adored. Right through his adult life Coöperation, temperance and the

Church were his dominating passions. He saw in them "the three great forces for the improvement of mankind." A man of titanic stature, and a bachelor, Mitchell lived in a small, plain, two-storied house in Rochdale even when "his" business was turning over £10,000,000 per annum. His house showed that "if he provided liberally for his friends he had no thought of himself. His own bedroom was furnished with some of the old furniture his mother had when he was a boy. Piles of reports and balance sheets took the place of ordinary literature." The description is from the pen of a well-loved friend, Sir William Maxwell (1841–1929), who was President of the Scottish C.W.S. from 1881 until 1908. Maxwell was a heraldic painter and an artist of merit. In his young manhood he had walked from Glasgow to London in search of work, tried to join Garibaldi's army, and had acted in a professional production of "Macbeth." His silver-tongued oratory on behalf of Coöperation was heard in every country of Europe (he taught himself French at the age of sixty-six when he became President of the International Coöperative Alliance) and in America and Canada, where he traveled from coast to coast in his seventieth year at the invitation of the late Earl Grey, then Governor General of the Dominions. These two men, both of whom died comparatively poor (Mitchell's estate realized £300), gave to Coöperation amazing enterprise and vision.

When Mitchell mounted the chair of the C.W.S. the Federation had reached a turning point in its history. Shrewd pursuit of Rochdale principles had carried the economies of the known market right over from simple retailing to the more complicated business of wholesaling. Why not production for this known market, coöperators were asking, and an extension, on behalf of consumers, of the successful principle? In answer to that challenge the C.W.S. had bought a biscuit bakery and a boot and shoe factory. Mitchell was to lead it into an extension of these activities and into the businesses of soapmaking, shipping, coal mining, tea growing, pottery, clothmaking, flour milling, cocoa manufacturing, textiles, cabinetmaking, tailoring, printing, and milk processing as well. All over England imposing C.W.S. warehouses arose. Depots were opened in America, on the continent of Europe and at focal trading points in the Empire. C.W.S. sales, under £2,000,000 in 1874, leaped to £4,700,000 in 1884, and approached £10,000,000 in 1894. Meanwhile, the Scottish C.W.S. had set out to smash "sweated" manufacture of shirts on Clydeside by producing for itself, and in 1887 opened Shieldhall, then and now the greatest center of productive manufacture in all Scotland. Boycott was one result of progress. Traders' Defense Associations raised the cry that coöperators did not pay income tax, and induced many private firms to dismiss from their employment workers who took their wages to the coöperative stores. Glasgow butchers closed the meat market to coöperative buyers. Later the rising Lever soap trust invoked the law, unsuccessfully, to prevent coöperators from selling the product of their own soap factories in their own shops. The tiny shops in Britain's back streets were showing too many consumers the better way to better business!

Suddenly, Liberal England faced a crisis. Unskilled labor was being organized in trade unions and, under capable, dramatic strike leadership, was impressing its plight upon the nation. Trade depression in 1890 was seen to be related to cyclical trade movements of which those of 1879 and 1886, when unemployment among trade unionists reached 10 per cent, were remembered vividly. Economists began to talk about overproduction; the wiser among them spoke of "underconsumption." Social legislation had not insulated the toiling millions against the dangers of a competitive system which piled up profits and converted them into capital goods at the expense of wages and consuming power. Men began to see unemployment as chronic and implicit in Capitalism.

A passion for social investigation swept the middle class. At the height of the 1886 depression a wealthy shipowner,

C.W.S. Cabinet Factory, Radcliffe, Lancashire

Scottish C.W.S. flour mill, Chancelot,
Edinburgh

Charles Booth, harnessed to social research the enthusiasm of comfortable young men and women whose aim was to uncover the facts of "the-condition-of-the-people" problem. Research lasted until 1903 and was published from 1884 onward in the classic volume known as *Life and Labour of the People in London*. It revealed that more than thirty in every hundred citizens of the world's proudest city were living in poverty. In 1899, during a period of exceptional trade prosperity, Mr. B. Seebohn Rowntree, head of a famous and respected business house, analyzed the condition of the people of York. Mr. Rowntree adopted as his minimum a diet less generous than that drawn up by the Local Government Board for workhouse inmates, allowing for a family of five 21*s*. 8*d*. per week, and making no provision whatever for amusements, beer, tobacco, newspapers, traveling or postage. He found 27.84 per cent of the whole population and 43.4 per cent of the wage-earning population living below this "poverty line." There followed a succession of similar investigations at Manchester, Middlesborough, Northampton, Reading and other typical towns. All of them underlined the indictment of Prime Minister Sir Henry Campbell Bannerman in 1903, that "there is about 30 per cent of our population underfed, on the verge of hunger . . . living in the grip of perpetual poverty."

Symptomatic of the social problem, although a special excretion of the factory system, was the evil called "sweating" against which, as we have seen, William Maxwell led Scottish coöperators. Small men, denied opportunities of engaging in industrial enterprise through lack of capital, set up in business in their own houses, putting unskilled labor to work at shockingly low wages and under disgusting conditions, upon the easily learned detailed processes of shirt, dress and millinery making. A short step from the home factories under one master was the conversion of the "sweater" into an entrepreneur, contracting out orders to individual women for completion in their homes. This work was irregular. Whereas a great factory bearing heavy overhead charges could close down only at great cost, the sweater's den could do business at the dictates of fashion or the caprice of the proprietor. As late as 1911, at the Coronation of King George V, the Union Jacks waved by a rejoicing people were produced in East End sweatshops by women paid at the rate of sixpence per gross. Moreover, the mass of misery represented in this type of industrial organization was a menace to the collective contract sought by trade unions. Women's work everywhere was ill-requited, especially in the tailoring, boxmaking, confectionery and laundry trades. At Cradley Heath, which Mary McArthur (1880–1921), organizer of the Women's Trade Union League, exposed as a burning sore, women forged chains for long hours at wages as low as 6s. 6d. per week, and from this pittance there was deducted 2s. for fuel and forge rent.

There was the 1906 Workmen's Compensation Act which improved and made permanent the Employers' Liability Bill of 1880. There was a series of statutes to provide the children of the poor with meals at schools and enforce periodical medical inspection of school children, founded on the report of the 1904 Commission on Physical Deterioration which established the existence of gross underfeeding. But the rising tide of legislation had failed to engulf the "sweater." Dispirited, Mary McArthur appealed to the editor of the Liberal *Daily News* to arouse the nation. Publicized by that newspaper, Sweated Trade Exhibitions, reproduced all over the country and supported vigorously by coöperators, whipped up a mass demand for reform. In 1909, a Trade Board Act, for the first time in the history of any capitalist State, made possible the regulation of hours and wages in industry. Where sweating was proved, the Act brought into being a Board endowed with legal power. In respect to chain-making the Trade Board established a fifty-four-hour week and, for women of eighteen years and over, a minimum wage of 11s. 3d.

Already, in 1906, coöperators had recognized the need for

a minimum wage. A coöperative employees' trade union (now the National Union of Distributive and Allied Workers) and the Women's Coöperative Guild, created in 1883 and still the only mass organization of working-class women in England, had secured the adoption by the Coöperative Congress of a wage scale providing for youths of fourteen 6s. weekly, rising in seven years to 24s., and for girls 5s. weekly, rising by annual increments to 17s. at twenty years of age.

Considerable trading success was attending coöperative effort. Under the impulse of departmentalization, retail societies were expanding consumer societies and facilities. New productive factories were being opened, every new move toward private monopoly, especially in articles of everyday consumption like soap, being countered by a fresh coöperative development. The Wholesale Federations of England and Scotland jointly acquired tea estates in Ceylon. The C.W.S. Bank was accepting individual deposits and enjoying large increases in its turnover. The Coöperative Insurance Society was brought into the joint possession of the two Wholesales. Immersion in trade problems did not divorce Coöperation from Trade Unionism, now a sharper spearhead than ever in the social struggle. From 1864 until 1912, the C.W.S. alone donated £26,000 to strike funds and funds for the relief of victims of depressed trade. Restless miners, whose fighting spirit even the sending of the military into Welsh valleys in 1911 could not break, won an eight-hour day and a Coal Mines Minimum Wage Bill after a succession of strikes in which the local coöperative stores were their commissariats and the Women's Coöperative Guilds were among their principal helpers. Railwaymen, too, when bringing the country to a standstill in 1911 as a protest against wage rates which outraged public opinion—forty in every hundred received 20s. or less each week—found in Coöperation a valuable addition to their reserve power. Working-class solidarity reached a climax in 1913 when a Dublin strike was met by police terrorism and attempts to starve the strikers and their children. Dublin became a beleaguered city. A call for help was transmitted to the C.W.S. by the Parliamentary Committee of the Trades Union Congress. In reply coöperators equipped two food ships with 50,000 bags of groceries and 50,000 bags of potatoes—the first of a contingent of eighteen food ships paid for by the Trades Union Congress—and broke the siege of Dublin.

Politically as well as socially and industrially, Liberalism was fighting a rearguard action. Invention was prolific in ideas pregnant with new and greater power. Electricity, the internal combustion engine, ships that sailed in the sky and under the sea—all these pointed to a land of promise; but the ranks of "clerks, agents, travelers, canvassers and others, whose tenure of employment is precarious, whose earnings are very low, and whose labour is largely waste" were swelling alarmingly, accentuating that hypertrophy of salesmanship which, like the rise of trusts, rings and combines, was demonstrating the difficulty experienced by a profit upon price system in disposing of its goods in poverty market. Sir Robert Peel, a Conservative, had broken the back of Toryism by embracing the Liberal doctrine of Free Trade. Now Joseph Chamberlain (1836–1914), a Liberal, made the first breach in the fortress of political Liberalism by propagating the Conservative doctrine of Protection, copying the elder Roosevelt's war cry of Tariff Reform for a precisely opposite purpose. To the left of Liberalism there thundered the great and growing political Labor army led by Keir Hardie (1856–1915), a fearless Socialist, attracting the loyalty of trade unions which hitherto had supported the Parliamentary candidatures of Liberal workingmen. In 1906, fifty-three Labor Members entered the House of Commons, making articulate the plight of the unemployed sections of an industrial society sickening under the blows of American, German and Japanese competition. The political temper of the times was indi-

cated in the Conservative campaign against Irish Home Rule
when politicians destined to reach the highest positions in the
State openly armed Ulster objectors and incited the army in
Ireland to mutiny. Home Rule, the battle for women's suffrage and the Liberal Government's attack on the House of
Lords' right to veto bills involving the expenditure of public money, diverted attention temporarily from "the condition of the people," which, Liberals could claim, was being
ameliorated by old-age pensions, by Labor (employment
finding) Exchanges, and by the National Insurance Act, providing a compulsory insurance fund, contributed by State,
employers and workers for the relief of the sick and unemployed. Yet these beneficent measures influenced but little
the living standards of the people in a period of sharp unemployment and rising prices. In 1911, five million out of eight
million workers were in receipt of less than 30s. a week, the
minimum wage below which stretched the poverty line.

Coöperation, capturing an ever-extending area of commercial enterprise from the thraldom of price upon profit, presented one of the few highlights in a somber picture. In 1913,
retail societies numbered one thousand three hundred and
ninety. Their three million members held £46,000,000 in
share and loan capital and reserve funds. They conducted a
trade of £83,000,000, yielding £13,000,000 of surplus, and
employed 103,000 workers at wages and under conditions
which were a model to their competitors. The two Wholesale
Federations, with capital resources of £10,000,000, had a
trade of £40,000,000, in which 32,000 workers were engaged.
The turnover of the C.W.S. Bank exceeded £169,000,000,
and the premium income of the C.I.S. stood at £223,000.
Congress had called for a survey to improve coöperative education, promote amalgamation among societies, and secure
standardized prices and dividends. If laissez faire was in
eclipse, Coöperation at least was preparing to greet a new
dawn.

Overnight, the black clouds in Great Britain's skies turned to red. Crude, competitive Capitalism moved swiftly to its final folly. The world battle for trade became a clash of flesh and blood. Europe was at war.

IV.

Plunge into Protection

COÖPERATORS responded immediately and magnifi-
cently to the country's cry for national service in
August, 1914. Before the year had reached its fear-
some end, revealing that a war which was to be "over by
Christmas" would become an exhausting struggle, £100,000
of coöperators' money, besides much relief in kind, had been
poured into funds to mitigate distress caused by death on the
Western Front and dislocation and unemployment on the
home front. Societies everywhere undertook to pay to dependents of employees who joined the Colors full wages "for
the duration," and promised to restore the volunteers to their
positions when hostilities ceased. Coöperative premises were
given up for billeting troops. Coöperative bakeries and factories were turned over to wartime production with speed and
efficiency. Hundreds of thousands of pounds of coöperative
capital were invested in war loans. Retail societies, following
the advice of the Coöperative Union, refused either to hoard
supplies of food or to advance prices, and played a vital part
in preventing panic. At a time when maximum prices were
the order of the day, the C.W.S. applied rigidly a policy of
minimum prices. While its prewar stocks lasted, it kept the
price of flour at prewar level. It sold Danish butter at 15s.
per hundredweight below prices obtaining in the open market. Its tea was invoiced at ½d. per pound below the regulation price. Retail societies could buy granulated sugar from
their own federation at 3s. per hundredweight below the price
fixed by the Government. When, in 1916, control of food
was effected and the ordinary channels of trade were used to
distribute supplies under the direction of the Government,
the C.W.S. was one of the few wholesale houses which elected

to accept the lowest rates of commission offered by the authorities.

Food control, indeed, was urged strongly on the Government by coöperators long before the German submarines made its application imperative. In March, 1915, the Parliamentary Committee of the Coöperative Congress asked the Government to tax all war profits to the fullest extent, to fix the prices of necessary foodstuffs, and to compel sales where hoarding was being practiced. Failing to impress authority, the Workers' War Emergency National Committee, comprising Coöperative and Labor representatives, urged the Prime Minister to (a) purchase all imported foodstuffs; (b) commandeer and control all home products such as meat, wheat, oats, barley, potatoes and milk; (c) commandeer ships and control freight rates (in the first twenty-six months of the struggle shipowners made profits of £300,000,000); and (d) place all supplies on the retail market at prices securing the full benefit of Government action to consumers. Yet every action of the Government seemed to indicate "a latent hostility" to coöperators, and an assumption that the only system for the distribution of commodities was that of the private merchant, wholesale dealer and shopkeeper.

The Sugar Commission, for example, decided its policy without consulting coöperators, the largest wholesalers and retailers of sugar in the land. Shortage of supplies to members registered through coöperative societies for meat, butter, margarine, sugar and potatoes was so chronic as to suggest that trade was being deflected deliberately from the coöperative store. The Coal Controller saw no reason in the Coöperative Movement's position as an important distributor to the domestic consumer to consult coöperative interests. In many districts the Movement was refused representation on war relief committees to whose funds it contributed generously. Some of these committees even refused assistance to applicants who possessed small capital resources in coöperative societies. When, in 1915, an Excess Profits Duty was imposed, it fell upon the surpluses of coöperative mutual trade, the Chancellor of the Exchequer pleading the nation's need in justification of a breach of the decisions of Committees on Income Tax, officials of the Board of Inland Revenue, and the law courts.

Most exasperating of all the results of maladministration was the treatment meted out to coöperative societies in 1916 when Great Britain's man power was conscripted and local military service tribunals were established to recruit men for the army. Local bosses, usually private traders, filled these tribunals, and used their position to cripple their coöperative trade competitors by refusing exemption to key employees. Indeed, the Parliamentary Committee of the Coöperative Congress reported in 1917 that "many cases have been brought to our notice in which it has been openly suggested by those in authority that coöperative societies were not entitled to the same consideration as ordinary traders." The consequence of constant irritation was to drive coöperators willy-nilly into politics. Swansea Congress in 1917 demanded coöperative representation on Government committees. A few months later an Emergency Congress declared for the formation of a Coöperative Parliamentary Representation Committee, which became at once active in the constituencies and emerged later as the Coöperative party.

Restriction upon its trade failed to retard the economic progress of Coöperation. Keeping down prices and devoting an ever larger proportion of their surpluses to reserve funds, retail societies were forced to reduce dividend on purchases. But fixed prices revealed to the consumer how real was the saving to their purses effected by the dividend, and membership leaped accordingly. By 1920, the prewar membership of retail societies had increased by one half. Retail trade had trebled, and amounted to £254,000,000. The C.W.S. had expended £1,500,000 in capital development. With its comrade federation in Scotland, it had acquired more tea plantations in Ceylon and broken fresh ground in India. Banking turn-

over exceeded £650,000,000. The premium income of the
C.I.S. showed a fivefold increase and reached £1,400,000.
The Movement's employees numbered 180,000 with a wage
bill of £12,000,000 per annum.

Impressive though these figures are, they pale into insig-
nificance before the astronomical inflation of the figures of private enterprise during the War. The day-to-day costs of the
War, comprising payments for soldiers' wages, food, clothing
and arms, and paid out of taxes and borrowed money, exceeded £7,000,000,000. Thus a prewar National Debt of
£700,000,000 stood in 1920 at £7,480,000,000. Wealth in
the hands of individual citizens after deduction of all taxes
(the Excess Profits Duty alone yielded £1,350,000,000) rose
by £5,000,000,000 over prewar fortunes. In 1920, two hundred and thirty-five private companies, with capital aggregating £98,000,000, distributed £65,000,000 among their shareholders in the form of bonus shares. Between 1913 and 1920,
Stock Exchange appreciations of oil, coal, steel, beer, shopping and clothing shares ranged from 182 to 731 per cent.
Trade combines, conceived long before 1914, were delivered in and nurtured by the limitless market provided by the
War Government. Prices were rendered rigid by the insistence of shareholders upon receiving the profits to which they
had become accustomed during four mad years.

Among the people discontent was rife. Wartime employment had brought hundreds of thousands of women into industry, increasing the number of wage earners per family, yet
wages had failed to keep pace with prices. In 1910 real wages
were 11.8 per cent below 1900 standard; in 1916 they were
30.1 per cent below 1900 standard; in the middle of the
boom of 1920 they were 7.6 per cent below 1900 standard.
A Coalition Government had extended the vote to women,
set in train a series of valuable educational projects and made
a tentative approach to tackling the slum problem. But war-
weary men were impatient for social change. The sky was filled
again with lowering clouds. Before the first quarter of 1921

sped by, a million idle men were walking Great Britain's streets. By the end of that year wages had fallen £315,000,-000. In 1922 wage cuts reduced mass purchasing power by a further £218,000,000. Railwaymen downed tools in 1919, forcing the Government to amalgamate competing systems into four great combines and improve wage rates. Miners threatened to strike in order to focus public attention on their plight and took their case to a Royal Commission which reported in favor of nationalization of the mines. The Government refused to implement its promise to give effect to the recommendation of its own Commission. Thus miners entered upon an industrial struggle which was to precipitate a National Strike five years later, and tragically embitter industrial relationships in postwar Britain.

The return of a Labor Administration in 1923 did little to improve the social scene. Great Britain passed into a period of rationalization with a permanent unemployed army of one million. Rationalization meant concentration of capital, the displacement of labor by machinery and further reductions of wages. By 1929, men hailed "recovery" with the permanent unemployed now two million strong. Then came the economic blizzard of 1931, freezing two thirds of the world's trade, sweeping a second British Labor Government into oblivion and sending the barometer of unemployment rocketing toward three million. Halt was called to expansion of social services, the way by which inequality of income might be assuaged and the State buttressed against decay. The national income was well sustained at £4,450,000,000 gross and £3,800,000,000 net after deductions for customs and excise and local rates (the taxes which provide the income of municipal and other local authorities); but its distribution bore almost the same relation to the various classes comprising the State as in 1914 or 1864. Two million three hundred thousand persons with earnings upward of £250 a year took £1,500,000,000. Five million seven hundred thousand persons earning from £122 to £250 a year took £1,030,000,000.

Twelve million persons, including neither the unemployed nor old age pensioners, had incomes below £122, and took £1,270,000,000. In brief, one in ten of the population drew £4 in £10 of the national income, while six in ten Britons drew only £3 of every £10 of the national income.

Not less significant than the maldistribution of income was the fact that 90 per cent of all economic activity in what was once the workshop of the world was destined for the home market. The Liberal vision of expanding trade horizons had faded. International trade, which implies exchange of the characteristic products of one country for the characteristic products of another country—in simple terms, division of labor—was dammed by tariff barriers. Henceforth division of labor, the productivity of which almost hallowed the Industrial Revolution, was to find expression in scientific management and in an intensification of industrial processes within the confines of the home market.

The slow, almost painful, growth of the "new economics" and their final overwhelming triumph in Great Britain is as interesting a story as any in history. In 1915 the Liberal Chancellor of the Exchequer closed Britain's shores to luxury imports as a wartime expedient. After the War these McKenna Duties were retained, the argument for their continuance being based upon the protection they gave to certain home industries and the revenue they returned to the National Exchequer. As public opinion became accustomed to this mild dose of Protection, there was propagated the idea of a Safeguarding of Industries Bill which had its roots in the Paris Economic Conference of 1916. Then, Allied statesmen, anticipating the fruits of victory, agreed "to render themselves independent of the enemy countries in so far as regards the raw material and manufactured articles essential to the normal development of their economic activity"; and wartime idealism was invoked on behalf of the Safeguarding of Industries Act in Britain—three years after the War! In a typical phrase, the Coalition Prime Minister, Mr. David

Lloyd George, himself a Liberal Free Trader, was able to acclaim Mr. Henry H. Asquith (later Lord Oxford) and Mr. Walter Runciman, both Liberal Free Traders, as respectively the wet nurse and father of Protection in Britain. For a period of five years, a duty of 33⅓ per cent of the value of various classes of goods produced in key industries was imposed. The Act did not apply to Empire imports. Under no circumstances was it to be extended to foods, drink and raw materials.

Part II of this same Act was designed to prevent the "dumping" in Great Britain of goods (other than articles of food or drink) at prices below cost of production or at prices which, owing to depreciation of foreign currencies, were below those at which similar goods could be manufactured profitably in the United Kingdom. In 1924, Mr. (now Lord) Snowden, and Mr. Sidney Webb, Chancellor and President of the Board of Trade in the Labor Administration, laid an ax to the roots of the McKenna Duties and Part II of the Safeguarding of Industries Act. Already, however, the British Labor Movement was divided on the Protection issue. A Keir Hardie would have cried: "A plague on both your houses! The poor are poor because they are robbed"; but trade unionists had joined employers in public pleas for tariffs on steel imports. With the voice of the consumer too small to be heard in the councils of the nation, the restoration of a Conservative Government in 1924 meant the immediate re-enactment and expansion of the Safeguarding of Industries Act.

Mr. Stanley Baldwin, while giving a pledge that Safeguarding would not be a wedge for general Protection, chose to introduce tariffs by the "White Paper Procedure," a simple extension of which in 1932 destroyed the last vestiges of Free Trade. An industry could apply to the Board of Trade for a duty. If the Board were satisfied that the claim had been substantiated, it referred the subject to an independent committee. This committee was charged with deciding upon the importance of the industry, its efficiency, the volume of labor it employed and so on, and with recommending the amount of the duty. When the Board of Trade and Treasury concurred in the report, the duty proposed was inserted in the Finance Act. Thus it required no special legislation, and was saved the cross fire of criticism in the House of Lords. This approach to Protection was tentative. In three years, out of fifty applications only twenty went to investigation and only nine were conceded.

Today, the approach by way of a White Paper Procedure is direct, and the result is almost certain. Applications are sent to an Import Duties Advisory Committee appointed by the Board of Trade and operating from permanent offices within sound of Big Ben. At the head of a long table there presides tiny, parchment-faced £7,000-a-year Lord May, ex-Chief of the Prudential Assurance Company, which has large investments in many protected trades. His lordship coughs dryly, adjusts his monocle and introduces his colleagues. On his right, silent and ascetic looking, is £5,000-a-year Sir Sydney Chapman, famous economist and advocate of Protection. On his left, sprawling, rotund and cheerful, is £5,000-a-year Sir Allan Powell, barrister, and a Protectionist of the "isn't-it-a-shame-the-Japs-can-sell-boots-here-at-less-than-we-can-make-them" school. Ranged along one side of the table are the applicants. Ranged along the other side are the objectors. At the bottom of the table are "other interests," as a rule rather inarticulate foreigners about to see their trade with Britain vanish. All sit on chairs made from imported wood. By the light of French chandeliers, all make their notes with lead pencils supplied for the purpose and stamped boldly "Empire."

Lord May tells everybody how friendly everybody is, and the debate opens. What capital is invested in the industry, what returns it obtains, what labor is employed and how many more could be employed given a tariff. Questions are asked. Lord May announces that, if a tariff is granted, the

Committee may exercise its power to insist upon the industry reorganizing itself efficiently, and may even withdraw the duty.

Later, the Committee reports to the Board of Trade and the Treasury, almost invariably in favor of a tariff. A Treasury Order brings the tariff into immediate operation. The Order lies on the Clerk's table at the House of Commons for twenty-eight days. Then the tariff is law, having acquired that dignity without the lobbying and logrolling which is so disgraceful a feature of legislatures abroad. Occasionally the tariff is revised—upward. Applicants, and they are not many, who are sent away empty on the first occasion can come again. The hearings are private. The one restraining influence is exercised by the Treasury: it prefers low tariffs to high. It still nurses the hope that exchanges may become free enough to facilitate foreign lending which absorbed one quarter of the national wealth in 1913 (£185,000,000) but only £53,000,-000 in 1934, and upon which rest the fortunes of the London money market.

To the tariff walls inclosing British shores there was added, in 1932, a ring fence round the Empire. The Mother Country, investing her surplus wealth in India, China and Japan, where "coolie" labor was ripe for exploitation at high rates of interest, had allowed America to conquer Britain in the self-governing Dominions. Three quarters of Canada's corporation shares were held by Wall Street. Australia was becoming dependent upon Uncle Sam for fresh capital. Now, in an effort to insure that, even if interest must follow the loan, trade would still follow the flag, an Imperial Conference at Ottawa concluded trade agreements which did not reduce Dominion tariffs on British goods but merely raised Dominion tariffs on other foreign imports.

Protection was but one facet of a many-sided expediency to sustain prices and profits. There was, for example, the direct subsidy policy endorsed by the Labor Administration of 1924 in the form of a subsidy to sugar beet growers. Why beet sugar should have been chosen for experiment is difficult to discover. To the argument that, in the event of war, sugar supplies might be cut off, there was the answer that cane sugar is capable of being stored in large quantities and for any length of time. To the statement that beet is a valuable rotation crop, there is the reply that for several centuries British agriculture had found this special crop of no special value. Against the subsidy, the case was overwhelming. Compared with cane sugar, available to Great Britain in her own Crown Colonies, beet sugar is poor in quality and uneconomic in cultivation. The creation of beet factories meant the destruction of existing refineries, ruin to the shipping which brought in cane from overseas, and distress in the Crown Colonies. Despite protests, the subsidy was approved for a ten-year period, the subsidy, plus remission of duty and excluding fluctuating subventions on molasses, being as follows: 1922–24, £1 5s. 8d. per hundredweight; 1924–25, £1 3s. 8d.; 1925–28, £1 6s.; 1928–31, £1 0s. 4d.; 1931–34, 13s. The Government itself bought shares in Home Grown Sugar, Ltd., guaranteeing interest at 5 per cent in a prospectus which contained the names of respected Labor leaders as directors. Inevitably, there was a rush by industrialists to produce at £1 5s. 8d. in Great Britain a hundredweight of sugar which could be bought from the Empire at 9d. The fact that many of these industrialists, because of the first postwar slump, were short of capital presented no bar to enterprise. Between 1921 and 1927, the Trade Facilities Acts raised £72,000,000 in loans for private enterprise, guaranteed by the Treasury as to principal and/or interest. Under these Acts £2,215,000 were advanced to sugar beet factories, of which only one third had been repaid when the subsidy completed its first ten-year trial. Eighteen factories capitalized at £4,500,000 were built. Their output capacity was 4,000,000 tons per annum, although the total consumption capacity of the country, including 300,000 tons of export trade, was only 2,200,000 tons per annum. In the result, the subsidy cost £42,000,000. At any given moment during its operation it amounted to 100 per cent of the value of imported sugar.

There was an interesting orientation of firms enjoying the bounty. One third of all the capital in the industry was held by foreigners, among them being Skoda, the Czecho-Slovakian armaments firm. A large share was held by the sugar distributive combine, Tate and Lyle, Ltd., who entered the business reluctantly, but found it a lucrative ancillary service. An Anglo-Dutch group, the English Beet Sugar Corporation, Ltd., to which the Government leased Home Grown Sugar, Ltd., because of colossal losses, achieved this remarkable record in the six years ended March 31, 1931: combined capital, £1,800,000; dividends paid, £1,303,000; depreciation, £1,192,000; placed to reserve, £960,000; six years' earning on £1,800,000, after paying income tax, £3,455,000.

Although Glasgow was famous as a center for the manufacture and export of sugar machinery, at least £1,023,000 of the plant bought by British companies came from abroad; some of it was reputed to be the second-hand discard of Dutch factories. The price of the policy did not end there. Imperial Parliament was forced to raise relief loans amounting to hundreds of pounds on behalf of the Crown Colonies.

This chapter on the art and science of subsidy might have been expected to close in 1934. It did not. There were then 366,000 acres under beet. Although the rate of assistance worked out at £300 per man employed per year, and the actual wages paid averaged only £80 per year, trade unionists clamored for continuance, covering the obvious charge that a swindle was being perpetrated under the parrot cry for nationalization. A vested interest had been created. The sugar capitalists, with the connivance of the Ministry of Agriculture, proposed a scheme for abolishing the direct subsidy but endowing themselves with a complete monopoly over sugar imports and placing, for ten more years, a levy of 2s. 4d. per hundredweight upon home consumption, thus yielding a new indirect subsidy of £4,000,000 a year. Amazing political stratagems were adopted to defeat the exposure of the sugar beet subsidy by the Coöperative Movement. Assistance was maintained at the highest rate for two years beyond the contractual period—bringing the total cost to over £50,000,000 —in the hope that opposition would fade and die. Ultimately, the factories were amalgamated (the market value of the most worthless of their stock appreciating) and a sharply falling rate of subsidy was guaranteed on a reduced acreage of beet, but in perpetuity.

Yet another aspect of Britain's "new economics" was the De-Rating Act of 1929, now costing a section of the community £33,000,000 a year. Certain local expenditure, it was claimed, had assumed a national character and ought to be transferred to the National Exchequer. The scheme was wrapped up in the garb of local government reform. It relieved "industrial hereditaments" of 75 per cent of their local rates, and agricultural land of 100 per cent of such rates. A bakery was relieved; a bread distribution depot was not relieved. Where the community gained by virtue of the proximity of the bakery to the distributive depot, neither was relieved since the whole failed to win recognition as an "industrial hereditament." One consequence is that many coöperative bakeries and dairies are paying 100 per cent of local rates and competing with private bakers and private dairymen paying only 25 per cent of local rates.

Food, however, still remained a problem in view of the pledges of politicians that there would be no stomach tax. Farmers pointed ruefully to the increasing mass of legislation underpinning the general price structure. They, who sold milk cheap, had to buy spades, saddlery and whatnot, dear. Between the price they received for their products and the price paid by the ultimate consumer, there was an enormous "spread." A Government Committee had revealed in

1923 that this spread was as high as 300 per cent for vegetables.[1] An effort to ease the farmers' plight was made by the Labor Government's Agricultural Marketing Act of 1931. Farmers then were invited to submit schemes for controlling the marketing, sale, grading, packing, storage, insurance, advertising, and transport of individual agricultural commodities. The aim was neither to cut prices nor to promote consumption. It was to increase the farmers' share of the "spread." The Act evoked no response. No scheme was submitted. The Conservative Government was not dismayed by this failure of its predecessor to enthuse farmers for Coöperation. It observed that, in relation to coal, Labor was committed to the principle of limitation of the market by means of quotas. The Coal Mines Act of 1930 sought to prevent cutthroat competition within the industry in relation to export trade. Selling agencies were authorized to allocate quotas of production to each pit, so creating a monopoly interest in the vague hope that miners' wages might rise. Here was the solution of the food problem. Quotas could be applied to agricultural commodities as a first instalment of Protection, disguised as reorganization. Marketing Acts so buttressed would be assured of success. A quota or proportion of the home market for bacon was allocated to home producers, no condition being made as to quality or price. Import quotas were fixed. Foreign importers in 1933 received £29,928,221 for 9,084,363 hundredweights of bacon. In 1934, under the quota scheme, they received £30,052,275 for 7,598,922 hundredweights. Inevitably the home producer failed to deliver his quota. Prices soared. The Stock Exchange valuation of shares in the bacon distributing combines soared in sympathy. Bacon disappeared from the poor man's breakfast table. The quota, however, had achieved its objective. It had driven up prices

1. This Departmental Committee on Distribution and Prices of Agricultural Produce met under the chairmanship of the Marquess of Linlithgow. It is referred to hereafter as the Linlithgow Committee.

and secured the establishment of a Pigs Marketing Board and a Bacon Development Board. Besides licensing producers, determining the conditions of their contracts with curers, and virtually closing the producing and curing industries to new entrants (the Bacon Development Board had acquired power to close existing factories altogether in 1938), these Boards provided railway companies with transport revenue in respect of pigs whether the pigs are carried to market or not, all the fresh overhead charges involved being unloaded on the consumer in prices. The Boards collapsed late in 1936—killed by their failure to guarantee consumers the right quality of bacon at the right price.

The Agricultural Marketing Act of 1933 covers milk, hops, and potatoes. Potatoes bear a tariff and are subject to quotas. A standard acreage is fixed and a fine of £5 is imposed for every additional acre brought into cultivation. The schemes are claimed as a form of producers' Coöperation. Their administration varies, but each Board receives its initial capital as a subsidy from the Government. It takes a note of all registered producers and, having obtained a majority in favor of organized marketing, it can compel the minority to accept its decisions. It fixes prices and derives its income from a levy on each pig or each gallon of milk. Consumers or distributors may protest. They have the right, if they have the money to pay for exercising it, to demand a public inquiry presided over by a lawyer appointed by the Minister of Agriculture or the Secretary of State for Scotland. When the chairman makes his report, the application of his recommendation is left to the discretion of the appropriate Minister. The results of the first two public inquiries initiated and sustained largely by the Coöperative Movement into prices fixed by the Milk Marketing Board reveal the value of this consumer safeguard. In one, the chairman reported that distributors and consumers had justified their complaint and that farmers' margins should be reduced. The Secretary of State for Scotland took no action. In the other, the chairman found that distributors' margins were excessive and recommended that the farmers' margins fixed by the Board should be sustained. The Minister of Agriculture took no action.

In the postwar years up to 1931, no less than £3,000,000,-000 was donated from the British Treasury in aid of private capitalist business. That sum included large-scale expenditure on unemployment relief, on public works, on subsidies to house building and similar semisocial services. As the costs of building material fell and it became possible to lower house construction costs without endangering land values, housing subsidies—paid to a considerable extent by super-taxpayers and, therefore, a method of redistributing wealth—were reduced almost to the vanishing point. Under the stress of the 1931 crisis, while industry was taken more and more into politics, the unemployed were thrust out of politics and economies were achieved at the expense of the recipients of public relief. Other forms of grants-in-aid were maintained almost intact. Capitalism went on the dole on a grand scale.

In Great Britain today, wheat production is subsidized. Herring fishing is subsidized. Cattle raising is subsidized. The production of oil from coal is subsidized. The building of ocean liners like the "Queen Mary," as well as tramp shipping, is subsidized. Civil aviation is subsidized. Armament manufacture is being subsidized to an extent never known in history. Duties upon food are £20,000,000 a year higher than in 1931. With import tariffs ranging from 10 to 50 per cent upon almost every commodity in use, indirect taxation increased by £85,000,000 in five years.

With the economic climate rendered so favorable to monopoly, opposition to the Coöperative Movement grew steadily in both virulence and vehemence. Important trading associations, formed to maintain prices, began to insist that the dividend was a mere rebate on price, that it involved price cutting and that, if the commodities controlled by them were to be sold in coöperative stores, the average dividend must be added to the price at the time of sale. The effect of this proviso was that a coöperative society paying an average dividend of 1s. 8d. per pound would either charge 1s. 1d. for a shilling article, or would refuse to include that purchase in the members' dividend voucher. If the society chose the first course the stigma of overcharging would be attached to all its transactions. If it chose the second course, the special attractions of "divi" were denied its salesmen. Soon manufacturers outside retail price-fixing rings, but afraid to offend private traders, began to apply the same policy to their trade with coöperative societies. The new services afforded by phonographs, radio and electric goods were closed to coöperative trade except on onerous terms. Where societies refused to accept such terms they were boycotted.

At the same time, London's West End stores were intensifying their competition by extensive development of mail order business. New distributive combines, like the Drapery Trust, sprang into life. Mighty concerns engaged in production began to branch out into retail trade. Woolworth stores and the shops of their British prototypes were bringing garish colors into village streets. The chain stores with highly specialized lines of goods were undercutting coöperative prices in one district, and recouping themselves at the expense of consumers in other districts where coöperative storekeeping was weak, or where societies tended to pursue a high price policy in order to maintain high dividends. The rapidly integrating relationship between retail business and great productive combines, and the encouragement given to trusts by the trend of legislation, are well illustrated in the returns of the Bacon Development Board for 1935–36. In that year the Board licensed 3,058 bacon-curing factories, 2,347 of which were branches of three multiple stores.

Gradually, with the assistance of the national Press, the campaign of attrition reached a climax in the demand that the special income tax position of coöperative societies should be reviewed and that there should be additional imposts upon coöperative funds. A Conservative Chancellor, under the pressure of the Association of British Chambers of Commerce, set up a Committee of Inquiry.

The case against the societies, separated from the special pleading and political propaganda which accompanied its statement, may be summarized as follows: they did not pay tax on surpluses deriving from trade done with nonmembers; sums not allocated to members as dividend on purchases but placed to reserve funds were not taxed; income arising from invested reserves also escaped liability. Therefore, coöperators were in a privileged position as traders and citizens.

The societies, answering that all coöperators paid tax upon their individual incomes and upon interest earned on their coöperative capital investments, met the specific case of their trade opponents in these terms:

Trade with nonmembers was negligible—in the case of the largest society in Scotland £400 out of £2,062,409, or less than .05 per cent—and societies generally paid a discount on these purchases. Surpluses arising from the activities of mutual associations organized not to make profits but to effect savings for their members were nontaxable and were recognized as nontaxable by the courts, by the Income Tax Act of 1918, and by the Industrial and Provident Societies Act of 1893 under which coöperative societies are registered. To tax coöperative reserve funds was to strike at this principle of mutuality, since the source of such funds was the same surplus of which the major share is distributed as dividend on purchases. The bulk of coöperative societies' investments is in other coöperative federations and is of the nature of a mutual interest. On their land and buildings coöperative societies pay tax at the highest rate although the incomes of the majority of their members are below tax exemption level. Whatever concession the societies did enjoy arose from arrangements to convenience the Treasury and were offset by their legal obligation to accept all the capital offered by their members and to pay a fixed rate of interest thereon—an obligation imposed on no enterprise registered under the Company Acts.[2]

The special case of the societies derived from the special nature of the campaign which forced the inquiry. They pointed out that, whereas there was no coöperator on the Committee, one of its three members was connected with a firm already boycotting coöperative societies by refusing to supply gramophones and gramophone records, and that this gentleman, in his evidence at the previous Government inquiry, had committed himself to the principle of imposing special taxation on coöperative funds. They complained that coöperative representatives were not permitted to cross-examine witnesses. More particularly, they resented the fact that an inquiry into industrial taxation should be confined to one section of the trading community.

The Committee reported unanimously in favor of taxing coöperative reserve funds. The Chancellor of the Exchequer included a special clause taxing societies at the rate of £1,-250,000 per annum in the Finance Act of 1933, although not before the Treasury had offered, privately, to lighten the impost on condition that coöperators withdraw their opposition; an offer rejected by the societies on the ground that they could not endorse any violation of the principle of mutuality. A protest petition signed by 3,346,755 electors—the biggest

2. The view of responsible members of the Inland Revenue Department was stated by the Deputy Chairman of the Board of Inland Revenue in 1904 thus:

"The fact remains that the operations of associations of consumers do not, to any appreciable extent, result in what may be called 'profits chargeable with Income Tax.'

"This becomes obvious when it is considered what would result if the societies, instead of charging, as they do, something like ordinary retail prices and distributing the savings in the form of 'dividend,' were to reduce their prices so that their takings just balanced their outgoings. There would then be no profit which could possibly be assessed. It would be absurd to argue that, merely because the societies, instead of realising their savings in the immediate form of low prices, choose to pay higher prices, and to make a distribution of 'dividend' once a quarter, the members have added to their taxable income."

protest petition ever organized—failed to influence Parliament. After a full-dress debate, the special coöperative tax became law.

The lessons of these events were not lost on coöperators. In the slump of 1921, their retail stocks depreciated in value and the price collapse lopped £35,000,000 from sales and £8,000,000 from surpluses. Booming business in 1920 had induced the C.W.S. to spend £700,000 for land and buildings—half as much in one year as it had ventured in the four war years of unparalleled prosperity. Now its trade fell by £24,000,000 and its accounts showed a deficit of £4,500,000.

The urgent need was for concentration and direction of resources. In the London area, where societies north of the Thames had been amalgamated and overlapping had been avoided between two mighty units south of the river, spectacular progress was demonstrating the practicability of amalgamation; but the natural fear of losing local autonomy threw up powerful barriers against intersociety action. Across these barriers, however, owing largely to the influence of the Coöperative Union, coöperative officials and committeemen were pooling business ideas. Better methods of stock control were discussed. More efficient statistical information was organized. Costs were analyzed. Salesmanship and publicity were considered more as a science and less as an unnecessary addition to overhead charges with which the known market should not be burdened. Every federation, trading and non-trading, was brought under microscopic investigation. While eighty years of cautious finance had secured the structure of Coöperation against the assaults of the severest slump in history, the slow growth of a new and more realistic spirit of collaboration enabled the Movement to resume its onward progress.

In 1929, before the price curve began its third great downward swoop of the postwar era, membership of retail societies stood at 6,100,000, share and loan capital at £128,000,000, sales at £216,000,000 and net surpluses at £26,100,000.

The next few years were to prove how definitely the Co-operative Movement was breaking the power of the price ring and the cartel and escaping from the thraldom of the capitalist profit upon price system. Coöperators went through the financial boom of 1929 without inflating the value of their enormous capital holdings by one penny piece. They emerged from the crash of 1931 without losing a single penny when, on the evidence of the Macmillan Committee on Finance and Industry, the capital of 284 companies registered in 1928 suffered a depreciation of 47 per cent. In the decade ending in 1935, the C.W.S. opened nearly forty new departments, factories and workshops exclusive of extensions to its existing premises. Despite a fall of approximately 36 per cent in wholesale prices, the value of supplies from its own productive works increased from £28,000,000 to £32,000,000. The story of the Federation's growth in 1935, when for the third successive year it expended more than £1,000,000 on capital development, provides an illuminating index to the Movement's method of meeting the new economic situation in Great Britain. Almost every one of fifteen milk depots was extended and equipped for manufacturing into tinned cream, condensed milk, butter and cheese, the growing "surplus" created by the operation of the Milk Marketing Board. Deprived under the Government's bacon scheme of supplies from its own Danish factories to the extent of nearly half their output, the Society quadrupled the output of bacon from its home factories, acquired a new factory and established new piggeries on its five estates. Incidentally, unlike many farmers who, given a monopoly, were careless of consumers' requirements and flooded the market with fat bacon, the C.W.S. designed its piggeries on the Danish model, which makes possible the economic production of pigs yielding lean bacon. To defeat the intensifying competition of the milling trust, the Sun Mills at Manchester were converted into the largest individual milling plant in Europe. Soap factories were reconstructed to increase their output of toilet soap and soap powder. The radio and electric rings were pierced by the direct manufacture of wireless sets, vacuum cleaners, electric irons and heaters. Manufacture of bicycles and clothing, canning and cabinetmaking, were all expanded. Fixed prices were applied over wider areas of trade, making possible more efficient organization of the mass market. Both in Scotland and in England, the Federations were recognizing that their very formation implied the delegation to them of the solution of thorny problems of business technique and leadership. The Highlands, stony ground for retail development even by chain stores, were opened up direct by the S.C.W.S., tiny societies fostered by them across the country from Stornaway to Peterhead winning a weekly turnover of £3,000. Right through the industrial Midlands of Scotland, milk creameries, laundries and funeral undertaking services, hitherto organized by small federations or left to the control of private combines, grew under the auspices of the S.C.W.S.; and that Federation is now contemplating the opening of retail shops specializing in the sale of drugs. The C.W.S. brought federal dairies under its control, and in 1936 gave a bold turn to its old policy of nursing weak retail societies back to strength by actually taking over Cardiff Coöperative Society, the first step in a plan to secure complete coöperative retail coverage of the entire country. In conjunction with the London retail societies it is now discussing the creation of a federation to meet the competition of the department store and the bazaar store. Coöperators may yet invade Oxford Street, London, and build cheek-by-jowl with Woolworth in the main streets of the metropolis.

Meanwhile the autonomous sections of the Movement were clamoring for unity. The annual Coöperative Congress, although still unable to enforce its decision even if it desired to replace voluntarism with compulsion, was nevertheless acquiring greater power. As part of a scheme of reorganization it created a completely representative National Authority charged with the task of expressing coöperative opinion on large questions of economic and political policy. The shouting and the tumult of the "Coöp tax" battle, which the Movement had lost, was over. Now coöperators prepared for war. In 1934, the Coöperative Congress called for a concentrated trade drive dramatized by a Ten-Year Plan. During each year until 1944, when the centenary of the Rochdale Pioneers will be celebrated, a new objective of membership and trade will be described. To each society will be allotted its own annual quota. How certain the response will be is indicated by the fact that in 1935 membership soared to 7,-500,000, an increase of 280,000 in one year and 70,000 over the quota; and retail turnover leaped to £220,000,000, an increase of £13,000,000 in one year and £400,000 over the quota. For 1936, the membership quota is 7,600,000. It will be exceeded. The retail sales quota is £232,000,000. It will be exceeded.

Grave though the charge may be that democracy in politics is inert, democracy in business is, clearly, on the move.

V.

The Dynamic of Dividend

EVERY minute of every day a British housewife enters a coöperative store, pays a 1s. membership fee which is credited to her capital account, and enjoys at once every advantage of coöperative trading. In November, 1925, Mrs. A joined South Suburban Coöperative Society. This Society pursues, deliberately, a low-price policy, and has habituated its membership to a comparatively low dividend. During eleven years, Mrs. A did not contribute one penny to her capital account beyond the 1s. membership fee, yet the sum standing to her credit in September, 1936, was £97 7s. 11d., all withdrawable at any time, plus £23 8s. due her in the event of her husband's death. Each half year, her dividend had been assessed and transferred to share capital account. Each half year, that account had been swollen by interest at a fixed rate plus the new increment of dividend. In eleven years she had accumulated a sum beyond the saving capacity of many British housewives during the whole of the normal working life of their husbands, and a sum which, had she exercised her purchasing power elsewhere, would have passed into the pockets of private shareholders.

The case of Mrs. A is not unusual. It is typical. Thousands of individual coöperators have saved in this way share capital holdings of £200, the limit permitted by the law affecting coöperative societies. Millions of individual coöperators have built up in this way whatever capital resources they possess. Of the £128,000,000 of share capital held by retail societies, 60 per cent is believed to be accumulated dividend. Here is one proof that dividend on purchases is the dynamic of the whole coöperative system.

Dividend is subject to criticism from two points of view.

The private trader argues that it accrues from inflated prices, that it represents the difference between the market prices charged by him and the alleged higher prices charged by coöperative societies. Many socialists also condemn the "divi" as a device for converting class-conscious proletarians into petty capitalists; they denounce coöperators, by and large, as "dividend hunters."

Take this second criticism first. It is surely an amazing confusion of thought that acclaims as noble the action of a bricklayer, *qua* producer, downing tools to enforce a wage increase of 2*s*. a week, but condemns as ignoble the action of that same bricklayer, *qua* consumer, spending his wages at his own coöperative store and, incidentally, stimulating the whole productive process, in order to obtain a saving of 2*s*. a week. The further argument of this school of criticism, that coöperative storekeeping merely economizes expenditure and so lowers subsistence wages to the great benefit of capitalists, is too reminiscent of Malthus to deserve anything but dismissal. It postulates that the more ignorant and poverty stricken the proletariat, the more certainly will they achieve their emancipation.

Look, now, at the argument of the private businessman. The kernel of his case is that beyond the margin between wholesale and retail prices, upon which he lives and upon which the coöperative system thrives, there is another margin, the result of overcharging, which contributes to the attractions of coöperative "divi." There are numerous answers to this argument, the majority of them provided by the businessman himself. He has formed price rings to impose minimum prices upon retailers. If the coöperative dividend did represent an addition to these minima, there would be no reason for the extensive boycott of coöperative societies by monopoly-seeking private business; and the very last thing private traders would desire would be the taxation of coöperative dividends. Again, every penny of coöperative turnover is earned in a keenly competitive trade offering con-

South Suburban Co-operative Society Ltd.

Registered Office:—69-71, London Road, Croydon.

In Account with ~~Ann~~ ~~·~~ ~~·~~

Share No. ~~·~~

Date.	Receiver's Initials.	Contributions.	Interest.	Dividend.	Withdrawals.	Fines.	Present Claim of Share Capital. Withdrawable.	Date.	Receiver's Initials.	Contributions.	Interest.	Dividend.	Withdrawals.	Fines.	Present Claim of Share Capital. Withdrawable.
20		1 0					1 0	Mar 26			1 10 5	5 2			79 18 7
12/26				1 11 3		N	1 12 3	Sept 4			1 12 11	4 5 6			85 14
9			6	1 16 3		EW	3 9	Mar 36			1 11 10	4 5 6			91 14 4
1/27			16	2 12		EW	6 2 6	W 5 36			1 14 1	3 19 6			94 4 11
8			3	1 19		EN	8 4 6								
14/28			4	3 9		EW	11 17 6								
6/28			56	3 9			15 12 0								
9	22 weeks		63	4 10			20 8 3								
7			10	5 6		EB	25 18 9								
6/30			12 6	4 4			30 15 3								
6			15	3 16 6			35 6 9								
7/31			17 6	3 18		A.O.	40 2 3								
5			1	3 12			44 14 3								
5/33			12	3 4 6			49 9								
3			14 6	2 4			52 19 3								
4/33			1 3 10	3 15			57 18 1								
2			1 3 9	2 15 6			61 17 4								
3/3			1 5 5	4 13			67 15 9								
1			1 7 11	4 2 6			73 6 2								

THIS BOOK SHOULD BE SENT IN FOR AUDIT THE FIRST WEEK IN JUNE AND THE FIRST WEEK IN DECEMBER.

Picture that tells the whole story. In eleven years "Mrs. A" has paid only 1*s*. (one shilling) yet has £97 7*s*. 11*d*. withdrawable at any time, to her credit. Dividend on purchases has contributed £78 14*s*. 6*d*. and interest on share capital (accumulated dividend) £18 12*s*. 5*d*. to her "nest egg." In addition, if "Mrs. A" becomes a widow, £23 8*s*. is due her as death benefit; in the event of her death, £11 14*s*. would go to her family.

Women's Coöperative Guild conference
in session

sumers every facility for deserting their own store if it fails
to satisfy as to price or efficiency. Many private traders, too,
from the great Lever Combine to the small corner shop,
have offered so-called "divi" to purchasers and have withdrawn these offers, presumably because the "divi" could be
earned only at the expense of profit.

What is the truth? Prevailing margins between wholesale
and retail prices enable coöperative societies to cover their
costs and make surpluses up to 10 per cent on sales. Societies
doing 66 per cent of all retail coöperative trade pay dividends
of 2s. or less. Societies whose trade is 23 per cent of the whole
pay dividends ranging from 2s. to 2s. 6d. Societies with 11
per cent of the trade pay 2s. 6d. or more.[1] Whether the
"divi" is high or low, however, its size is determined by the
member-consumers of each autonomous democratic retail society. In some parts of Lancashire, for example, consumers
regard coöperative storekeeping in two ways: (a) as a method
of securing for themselves the margin between wholesale and
retail market prices less costs of distribution, without relation
to the normal weekly saving which consumers, as house-
holders and citizens, must effect from wages to meet future
commitments like rent, rates and holidays; and (b) as a
method of saving, by paying higher prices, to meet these
future commitments. In other words, they use their coöperative society both as a store and a bank. "A" equals pure
dividend. "A" plus "B" represents high dividend deriving
from high prices. But the existence of the increment we have
described as "B" does not invalidate the claim that "A" is a
clear gain to the consumer. "B" indeed, is akin to the rebate
upon purchases which private companies, in an effort to defeat
the attraction of pure dividend, offered consumers but which
they found it impossible to sustain for this simple reason:
whereas they compelled their customers to provide the profit
fund from which this rebate derived (or else deprived their

1. G. Darling, *The Economics of Coöperative Trading.* A paper read to the
British Association (Economic Section), September, 1936.

shareholders of interest on capital, an illegal, not to say immoral, practice in capitalist organization), this extra surplus in coöperative trading results from the voluntary decision of consumer-members at the balance-sheet meetings of their own societies.

Having cleared the ground of its undergrowth of misconception, it is possible to discuss how coöperative surpluses are, in fact, distributed, what economies they reflect in retail and wholesale trade and in coöperative production, and what is their real significance in the modern economic system.

A study of the balance sheet of any retail society reveals that coöperators deduct depreciation allowances before arriving at their net surpluses, and these allowances are usually on a very liberal scale. Typical rates are: land, 1 per cent per annum; buildings, 2½ per cent; fixtures, 5 per cent; and machinery, 7½ to 20 per cent. The effect of this generous allowance for depreciation is that many coöperatively owned properties are worth far more on the market than their value in the books of coöperative societies; they constitute an important, although unknown, hidden reserve contributing to the enormous financial stability of the whole Coöperative Movement. Of a similar nature is the allocation to reserve funds, varying according to the prosperity of the society. Total reserves exceed £12,000,000 and represent nearly 10 per cent of the share capital—a high proportion of interest-free capital. Insurance is charged as in any private business, but there is one difference. The majority of coöperative societies allocate one penny per pound of annual sales as a premium, administered either by the society itself or by the Coöperative Insurance Society, to a scheme of collective insurance. Under this scheme, all coöperators are secured in respect to death benefit. When a member dies, his purchases are averaged over three years, and a sum amounting to 4s. per pound for a married man, widower or single person and 2s. for a married woman, is paid to the dependents. These death benefits aggregate over £500,000 each year. Although not accounted as such, they are a clear addition to dividend upon purchases. To the Coöperative Union goes 2*d*. per member. To education—men's and women's guilds, study groups and cultural classes all representing social services available to all who care to enjoy them and, therefore, another form of dividend—and to charities, including coöperative convalescent homes, there is donated £300,000 a year. The remainder is the net surplus. From it is paid interest on capital and dividend on purchases.

The paucity of information about private business makes comparison between the coöperative "divi" and private profits difficult. Coöperators calculate dividend on sales. Private business calculates profits on capital. As we have seen, coöperative societies are bound by law to accept and pay interest on all capital offered them by their members up to the individual limit fixed by their rules and not exceeding £200, an obligation from which private business is free. But against the 10 per cent on ordinary shares returned by the great grocery combines in 1934, there may be set the "divi" of £26,000,000 which, if distributed as interest on share capital, would have represented a return of 20 per cent, and, if distributed on the actual amount of capital used by societies in their own stores and wholesale federations (£80,000,000), would have represented a return of 32 per cent. These figures are affected by several factors. The main rivals of the Coöperative Movement organize mass sale of a comparatively small range of specialized commodities. Coöperative societies, however, seek to sell as wide a range of commodities as possible, varying though their profit margins may be. This is a vital consideration. Gross surpluses per pound of sales on different cuts of bacon alone may range from 21.4 per cent to 33.3 per cent, and on sugar may be regarded as satisfactory at 4.25 per cent. Moreover, the chain store with no special local interest to serve will plant a branch only in a district most likely to yield the highest gross surplus. The coöperative society has a local interest to serve. Its first care is the needs of its members and not the profits of shareholders. It must meet every demand, whether of "cash-and-carry" trade in crowded city areas, or of delivery trade in outlying, sparsely-populated areas, whatever the gross surplus yielded by these differing types of trade may be. This is not to suggest that chain stores do not meet both these types of demand and the many others in between. The point is that they need not, and the coöperative society must, meet them.

It is doubtful if the allowance for depreciation in the general distributive trade is as generous as in coöperative societies. It is certain that nowhere in the distributive trades are there such consumer services as collective life insurance and educational facilities, costing the Coöperative Movement a round million pounds sterling each year and charged against the expenses of business.

Finally, there are labor conditions. Labor standards in the Coöperative Movement are incomparably better than those obtaining in private trade. Indeed, the Minister of Labor himself, in an endeavor to rescue the distributive trade from the charge that it is a sweated industry, has suggested (October, 1936) that long hours and low wages are a recognized form of competition maintained at the expense of the workingpeople. It can be stated without fear of contradiction that sweating of employees is repugnant to coöperators and unknown in their business. Over the whole field of distribution, coöperative employees are better remunerated than their fellows in private employment, their numbers bear a smaller proportion of lowly paid juniors and their hours of labor, 48 per week, and in many stores 44 per week, are fewer. For the great majority of them, too, there are superannuation schemes providing retiring allowances. Whereas distribution, "labor turnover," is notoriously high, in the Coöperative Movement "labor turnover" is almost nil.

Does that 10 per cent on sales called dividend spell efficiency? Records of relative efficiency are hard to find. In Great Britain, however, the conclusions of a series of governmental inquiries into many aspects of commerce have been published in official reports, or Blue Books. We shall have occasion to refer to these reports later. Meanwhile we may look at the situation in the coal trade. The report of the Royal Commission on the Coal Industry (1926) summarized a comparison between the costs and profits of six private London coal merchants and a typical coöperative society. The private figure for the cost of the coal per ton and depot charge was 35s. 3d. against the coöperative figure of 33s. 1¼d. Private cartage expenses were 5s. 7½d. against the coöperative 7s. 11½d., the advantage of the private merchant being occasioned by his sales to industrial concerns and large consumers, whereas the coöperative trade was almost entirely with very small domestic consumers. Private establishment, clerical and other charges were 4s. 6½d. against the coöperative 3s. 5½d. To the basic coal cost of 35s. 3d. the private merchant, therefore, added 10s. 2d. plus a net profit of 6½d., selling at 45s. 11½d. per ton. To the basic coal cost of 33s. 1¼d. the coöperative society added 11s. 5d. plus a net profit of 11½d., selling at 45s. 5¾d. per ton. Besides retailing at 5¾d. below the private merchant the coöperative society showed a larger profit, the bulk of which was returned to the consumer as dividend. The conclusion drawn by the Commission was that "if all the retail trade in London could . . . be conducted as economically as that of the coöperative society . . . a very substantial margin would be available, either for reducing prices to the consumer, or for increasing prices to the colliery, and so increasing wages to the miner."[2]

What are the elements of economy in Coöperation? How is it that during the last ten years the Movement has been able to spend many millions of pounds on developing new factories and opening thousands of new branch shops, make ample provision for depreciating the book values of its properties, offer social services worth many more millions of pounds to its members, and return to consumers "divi"

2. Command Paper 2600, p. 89.

amounting to £245,000,000? There is the fact of dividend itself, an advertisement of enormous value, and contributor-in-chief to the known, nonspeculative market for which the retail store caters. Coöperative enterprise bears none of the costs of capital promotion. The Movement has no difficulty in obtaining a plentiful supply of cheap capital. It issues no prospectuses. It pays no underwriting fees. It offers no inducements to speculating investors. These virtues of retail Coöperation apply also to its wholesale trade. Roughly two thirds of all the commodities on the shelves of retail stores are bought from federations like the C.W.S. The C.W.S. works for a market in which changes are the changes of growth. It earns the "spread" between production costs and wholesale prices, this spread being increased by its power to purchase in bulk for a well-measured market. It makes the same charges against its earnings as any retail society. It returns a net surplus to retail societies as interest on capital and dividend on their wholesale purchases, the "divi" being 4d. per pound on all trade, plus an additional 3d. per pound on trade in the Federation's own products. Now, in actual practice, retail societies seldom call upon their C.W.S. receipts to meet interest charges on their own capital. Just as the individual coöperator allows a large proportion of his dividend to accumulate in the funds of the retail societies, so the individual retail society allows its dividend to accumulate in the hands of the Wholesale Federation. Indeed, it is estimated that if retail societies took into their distributed profits income from invested reserves and from subscribed capital, reinvested mainly in the C.W.S., their capital charges would amount to less than 1 per cent of their aggregate sales. It may be questioned if any other retail business in the world operates at so low a capital cost.

The flow of goods from Wholesale Federation to retail store occasions important financial transactions. These are centered in the C.W.S. Bank. Like other coöperative federations, the Bank also returns its earnings to the coöperative

London offices of the C.W.S. Bank

London headquarters of the C.W.S.

pool. Its operations mean that between the local store and the federal warehouse there are no bad debts. All goods are automatically paid for on delivery. There are no credits placing fresh interest burdens on coöperative commerce.

Take another step back—or forward—to production. There, similar economies are effected. The C.W.S. produces to meet a known market. It runs little danger of losses from unsold stock. As a result, coöperative wholesaling costs amount to only 2.3 per cent of sales. To this very low charge there is added another 1.5 per cent representing interest upon capital, substantial provision for reserves and depreciation and dividend upon purchases. Over a very large proportion of their supplies coöperative retail stores buy more cheaply from their own Federation than they or any of their rivals can buy elsewhere.

It is these economies beginning in the retail store, and proceeding to wholesaling, production and finance, that are returned ultimately to the consumer, by whose simple act of collective spending a mighty movement is galvanized into activity.

In the Forties of last century, as we have seen, workingmen reformers were seeking as trade unionists and consumers a new contractual relationship with capitalist society. While the trade unionist has won recognition for his contract, the duration of the contract remains a matter of chance. New industries, new orientations of old industries, the appearance of new classes of worker engaged on repetitive processes, and the disappearance of old types of craftsmen have affected the value of his contract. Indeed, the exercise of his political power now influences more profoundly the development of industry, and does more to promote equity in the distribution of industry's reward than so-called "direct action." The progress of the consumer has been different. He has proceeded from contract to conquest. He has learned how to supersede the entrepreneur and the middleman. He has released himself from the grip of the capitalist and the toll of the usurer.

He has himself become a landlord, although on a small scale. Here is the basis of hard fact upon which fantasy may build the State of tomorrow—a State in which the consumer-laborer owns all land, controls all capital, and organizes all commerce to produce for the known market; a State in which cyclical fluctuations in trade and employment are ironed out, and social dividends are earned for the enrichment of all citizens. Meantime, in the world of day-to-day business the Coöperative Movement is a state within the State. It has solved the problem of "saving," which economists have found so insurmountable a barrier to the success of Collectivism, and it has relegated capital from a position of overlordship to the role of servant in industry. Coöperative dividend creates capital goods, but it also increases purchasing power and expands the market, which brings to fruition the combination of saving and labor in industry, for the nature of coöperative dividend is threefold. There is a dividend yielded at the moment of purchase in the form of lower prices or higher qualities, or both; there is a dividend amounting to 40 per cent of retail surpluses accumulated for six months, then spent on consumers' goods; and there is a dividend, 60 per cent of the whole, allowed to accumulate for longer periods but called on either in time of emergency, or to buy houses, provide holidays, or ease the old age of its consumer-owners.

During the last fifteen years the number of persons absorbed into all industry has risen by 23 per cent. In the Coöperative Movement over the same period the number of persons absorbed into employment has risen by 47 per cent. This state within the State is a land without unemployment. Coöperation has shown that demand can be measured and that the waste of speculation in organizing production can be eliminated. It has shown that dividend upon purchases can insure that balance between investment and expenditure which stimulates maximum economic output. If, in the coöperative state of tomorrow, increased savings or capital are desired, the dividend rate can be adjusted to secure that result.

If larger expenditure on consumers' goods is desired, dividend can be paid in vouchers exchangeable for commodities, and the virtue of thrift will cease to imply the vice of hoarding. In practice, "forced spending" will be unnecessary. The conversion, through the more equitable distribution of spending power, of Britain's poverty market into first a prosperity market and then a quality market, on expert evidence, would raise the demand for food by £200,000,000 a year at present retail prices, would double the market for clothing, treble the market for furniture, hardware, crockery and household goods, and stimulate even larger demands for houses, tobacco, drink, confectionery, travel and entertainment.

For a long time ahead, however, the Coöperative Movement will be concerned less with toppling magnates and millionaires from their thrones than with rescuing the multitude from the ever-present menace of pauperism. The "divi" will continue to be the dynamic of coöperative effort in the humbler task of controlling price levels and checking the excesses of monopoly. The speed with which the position of the organized consumer changes from one of passive protection to one of active control of production depends upon the skill with which Great Britain's 1,100 autonomous coöperative societies concentrate their giant strength in pursuit of that immediate purpose.

VI.

Business Democracy at Work

THE consumer is a Forgotten Man of Commerce. Years of persuasion, through countless books on economics and trade newspaper articles, were required to win acceptance for the view that the function of distribution is part of the process of production. Even now politicians and economists consider the consumer a mere abstraction. Land, labor, capital and organizing skill—the factors of production—are for them the eternal and only verities, and the real subject of political economy. Under these circumstances, it is not surprising that businessmen in search of profit, the motive of supply, should be blind to this fact; that supply can provoke an incurable congestion, like stone dust in the miner's lungs, unless consuming power, the dynamic of demand, is widely and equitably diffused. Like the businessmen, economists and politicians visualize society as a series of *group* relationships in which the so-called factors of production occupy places won by their relative bargaining power and the consumer occupies no place at all. Thus private enterprise, in its organization, becomes as impersonal as its tools of production. While it accumulates property in the hands of the individual, it destroys individuality. No vital personal interest is represented in the administration delegated by absentee shareholders to clerks, accountants and managers. Business, in the words of the socialist critic, is a mighty amorphism, without a soul to be saved or a body to be kicked.

Now, it is the task of the Coöperative Movement, while diffusing wealth, to create and encourage individuality. When a man joins a coöperative society he becomes something more than a participant in the benefits of collective trading. He becomes an active partner in the conduct of the world's biggest Big Business. Coöperation places no money bar in the way of exercise of individual ability. There are no cash qualifications for coöperative directors. There are no stipulations against the individual with a flair for management. He need only win the confidence of his fellows to have open to him positions of responsibility and importance.

At the half-yearly meeting of a retail coöperative society a democratically elected committee presents to the members a balance sheet which, in its detail and simplicity, leaves few secrets locked in the breasts of administrators. It opens, usually, with a review of the state of trade and employment in the society's area and a note on new governmental legislation affecting coöperative development. It records the attendances of committee members at committee meetings. It reveals the society's financial position in trade, investment, revenue and profit and loss accounts, indicates the turnover in each department and in every branch store (with a comparison for the corresponding trading period), recommends the way in which the realized surplus should be distributed, and ends with an auditor's certificate. Few items escape the scrutiny, often highly expert, of the assembled consumers who, in their private capacity, are butchers, bakers and candlestick-makers. Housewives condemn the price charged for this commodity, commend that service. The general manager or secretary (frequently one official combines the two offices in a managing secretaryship) submits himself to cross-examination and the enjoyment of personal contact with his customer-employers.

Then come elections. In the larger societies the records of candidates are printed and circulated. In all societies voters know with some intimacy the characters and capacities of the men and women seeking their suffrage. Like other electorates, they may, and do, err in assessing the quality of those to whom they commit the care of their personal savings and collective property. But they cannot choose money grabbers; the rewards of coöperative committeemen are fixed by rule. They cannot give power to financial speculators; coöperative business knows no speculation.

The committee divides itself into subcommittees concentrating upon finance, grocery, drapery and other departmental services provided by the society. Each subcommittee meets regularly with the appropriate manager to transact the business of its department. A full committee meeting is held at intervals, under the guidance of the general manager, to review every aspect of the business, to determine policy and to decide on new development schemes. All this work, virtually, is voluntary. Committees of management—sometimes they are called boards of directors and Scotsmen, especially, have a fondness for this grandiose designation—are paid small fees, allowances for time lost from their employment when engaged on society business, and traveling expenses, all fixed by rule and subject to the approval of the members. Curiously enough, committee members are permitted no monopoly of delegations to the quarterly meetings of the C.W.S. and the S.C.W.S., the national parliaments of democracy in business. A retail society delegation of four to a C.W.S. meeting will comprise, as a rule, two nominees of the committee of management and two persons elected by the members of the society. The aim is not to put a brake on directorial indiscretion. It is to bring as large a number of individual coöperators as possible into contact with the problems of business and to sustain that volume of well-informed criticism which is the breath of life to democracy.

The C.W.S. is a retail society "writ large." Retail societies subscribe to it one £5 share for every two members. They exercise one vote by virtue of membership, one vote in respect of £10,000 of annual trade with the Federation, and one vote for each £20,000 of trade above the first £10,000. Thus a retail society sending four delegates to C.W.S. meetings would need to trade with its own Federation to the extent of £50,000 per annum. Power in the Federation does not follow shareholding. Like dividend on purchases, it follows trade loyalty.

The C.W.S. is divided into three districts and its directors, although chosen by national vote, are representatives of these districts. Fourteen are nominated by retail societies in the Manchester area, six by societies around Newcastle and eight by societies in London and the South. Within these three districts, eight quarterly divisional meetings are held on the same Saturday, a similar agenda being submitted to each and the votes cast being totaled. On the following Saturday a final meeting is held in Manchester, votes are aggregated and decisions put into effect. C.W.S. directors give full-time service and receive salaries commencing at £750 and rising to £1,000 a year. (S.C.W.S. directors are paid £500 per annum.) They are eligible for reëlection every four years and retire on superannuation at the age of sixty-five. Their duties, subdivided like those of committee members of retail societies, take them all over the world: buying for 171 factories, inspecting farms and sales rooms, examining new plants, exploring new services, acting as liaison officers between department and department and between the management and their constituent members.

In the very search for supplies, the C.W.S. is a missionary of the coöperative idea. As an importer and exporter, it seeks, naturally, to deal directly with coöperative organizations overseas, to extend to them the benefits and obtain for itself the economies of the known market. Its exports to coöperative societies exceed £600,000 a year. Its imports from farmers' coöperative societies exceed £1,000,000 annually. By financing, on easy terms, the output of West Australian wheat growers and other Empire farmers, and setting an example which the Commonwealth Government has now followed, the C.W.S. released producers from the grip of the money monopoly. In its relations with the Coöperative Farmers' Organization of New Zealand it brought this consumer-producer relationship to its highest form of development. The

New Zealand Produce Association, owned jointly by the
C.W.S. and the Coöperative Farmers, marketed New Zealand
Farm Produce in Great Britain. The C.W.S. having bought
what it required, the remainder was sold on the open market.
All surpluses were divided between the C.W.S. and the New
Zealand Farmers; they were shared equally by producers and
consumers. An important volume of trade (£443,440 per annum) was placed beyond the grasp of middlemen and monopolists. Much of it was withdrawn from the profit-upon-
price system. It was freed from speculation, a root cause of
overproduction which ruins the producer; and this evil was
eliminated without recourse to restriction of supply, which
robs the consumer.

Besides the national coöperative federations of England
and Scotland, there are numerous local federations, all organized by retail societies and controlled by and for the consumer. Federal expansion, economically and historically, is
the coöperator's answer to private capitalist concentration.
Having measured its market, a retail coöperative society may
decide that that market does not constitute an economic unit
for milk supply. Then the known market of one society may
be linked with the known market of a neighboring society,
or a number of neighboring societies, the whole being supplied by a federal dairy. There are also federal laundries,
coal societies, funeral furnishing societies, boot-repairing
factories and bakeries.

Among the most interesting of these local federations is
the United Coöperative Baking Society, operating in Glasgow the biggest baking plant in the British Empire, and having several branch bakehouses besides. To meet the competition of chain stores in the confectionery business, the U.C.B.S.
engages in retailing through well-appointed shops. The
shopper at these federal stores receives a voucher recording
the amount of his purchases and is paid a dividend thereon
by his own society, which recovers this from the Federation
at the end of the accounting period. Another feature of the

federal principle is shown in the boot and shoe, clothing, printing and a few miscellaneous factories, owned jointly by their working people and retail societies, and organized in the Coöperative Productive Federation. These semiself-governing workshops are the historical survivors of the ventures in industrial democracy sponsored by the Christian Socialists, and are still claimed by their adherents as the real repositories of the ideal of "coöperation for self-employment." Workers share, in the form of bonus on wages, and consumer societies through a dividend on purchases, the surpluses of forty-four factories having an annual output worth £3,000,000. Their value to the Coöperative Movement is that they provide a check against dangers of overcentralization and lack of specialization in catering to individual demand.

Let us return now to the consumer in the retail society, the small man who capitalizes this group of businesses, controls them, enjoys their bounty and has proved himself to be brilliantly enterprising in associated effort. His is "a business with an idea." He capitalizes collective good will in pursuit of social aims, in much the same way as he coördinates consuming power in pursuit of dividend. At his quarterly business meeting he reviews the affairs of an educational committee, possibly also of a political committee, charged with promoting the social and cultural interests of coöperators. There are classes for employees, study groups, choral and dramatic associations and sports clubs. Some societies center these activities in a "home," usually a mansion acquired and developed as a place of rest and leisure. Besides enjoying local autonomy, many of these agencies have built up national organizations exercising influence on the life of the State. The Women's Coöperative Guild is an outstanding example of this type of organization, arising spontaneously from the desire for social expression of an economic practice, fostered by the Coöperative Movement but essentially self-supporting.

The Guild provides an invaluable field for experiment. Its reactions to new services and to the products of existing factories are important to coöperative officials. Its knowledge of the working-class woman's domestic problems has enabled it to advise the Coöperative Movement on the peculiar forms of hire-purchase adopted to meet the competition of drapery and furniture chain stores. In its branches, thousands of women have been trained to take their place with men in the administration of coöperative business; one guildwoman has served as a full-time director of the C.W.S. The Guild's more spectacular achievements, however, have been in the wider sphere of citizenship. Its leadership made votes for women as vital a subject of debate at the firesides of the working classes as it was in the drawing rooms of middle-class suffragettes. Today, hundreds of guildwomen are to be found serving the community on local government bodies. The reforming zeal of coöperators on behalf of the woman wage earner springs from the continual pressure of the Guild. A successful campaign, first for the inclusion of maternity benefit in the National Health Insurance scheme and, later, for the payment of that benefit direct to the childbearer as a right of motherhood, stands to the Guild's credit. Its most recent effort has been the collection of working-class budgets upon which Sir John Orr and other nutrition experts based their searching inquiry into "Food, Health and Income," and aroused Parliament to the fact that one half of the British population is not getting enough of the right kind of food to eat.

The Women's Coöperative Guild proceeds from the local branch to district associations which coördinate its activities over small areas, right up to Sectional Councils operating in great areas, and thence to a Central Committee with permanent offices and secretariat. All its officials are popularly elected. Its policy, which treats of food standards, nursery schools and world peace, and touches life at every point, is formed by its own annual congress, but on essential matters is in accord with the policy of the Coöperative Union. The Guild is a microcosm of that full and vigorous democratic life of which the Coöperative Union is the macrocosm.

From its Manchester headquarters, the Coöperative Union reaches out to the smallest, most remote retail societies and to all their agencies. This it does through nine sectional boards with skilled officers, which cover Great Britain and devolve, by way of district associations, to local management committees, educational committees and even smaller units in the coöperative State. In its national affiliations, the Union includes the Wholesale Federations, the Coöperative Productive Federation, the Coöperative Press and the Coöperative party. There is no phase of coöperative effort outside its purview, whether it be the administration of one of the convalescent homes coöperators have built for their members, the expansion of the trade of a society with fifty members and one branch store or the transactions, amounting to £2,-000,000 a day, of the C.W.S. Bank. The task of the Union is to unify all coöperative action for the realization of the idea behind coöperative business, expressed thus in its constitution:

. . . to promote the practice of truthfulness, justice, and economy in production and exchange.

(1) By the abolition of all false dealings, either

(a) *direct*, by representing any article produced or sold to be other than what it is known to the producer or vendor to be; or

(b) *indirect*, by concealing from the producer any fact known to the vendor material to be known by the purchaser to enable him to judge of the value of the article purchased.

(2) By conciliating the conflicting interests of the capitalist, the worker and the purchaser through the equitable division among them of the fund commonly known as *Profit*.

(3) By preventing the waste of labor now caused by unregulated competition.

The Union operates through several departments, all of them growing steadily in scope and importance. There is a

Legal Department devising model rules, and interpreting legal formulæ in terms of coöperative practice. Where necessary, the Union contests legal decisions in the courts. In addition to administering Union finances and many special funds, a Finance Advisory Department provides advice on taxation, rating and valuation problems, and keeps coöperative accountancy methods under constant consideration with a view to improvement. A Labor Department drafts agreements with trade unions, collaborates with District Hours and Wages Boards and Sectional Councils, and is a party to the National Conciliation Board for Coöperative Service, which has brought industrial arbitration to a reasonable level of perfection and rendered the Coöperative Movement almost immune to strikes and lockouts. This Department seeks to popularize principles like superannuation for employees and collaborates in campaigns to improve labor standards outside as well as inside the Movement. An Agricultural Department gives service to societies engaged in farming, keeps a sharp eye on legislation affecting primary commodities and is, in fact, the only adequately informed voice in Great Britain correlating the interest of consumer and producer in agricultural affairs. An Education Department, with a full time Adviser of Studies and a growing teaching staff, conducts national examinations for standard courses in business and management (taken by over 52,000 students), provides correspondence tuition in cultural as well as business subjects, runs a Coöperative College and organizes summer schools and week-end schools for officials, employees, committeemen, juniors, adolescents and women. The Statistical Department is an office of increasing value, and a fully equipped Research Department is a recent addition. The Joint-Parliamentary Committee, stating the Movement's case at Government inquiries and giving day-by-day expression to coöperative opinion on economic and political matters, is the brain of political coöperation, while the Coöperative party handles propaganda and education and relations with its constituency. This, the youngest of the political parties in Great Britain, is a department of the Union; but it holds its own annual conference, and its income is derived from the voluntary contributions of affiliated societies with five million members. It is in alliance with, but not affiliated to, the Labor party, has nine M.P.'s in the present House of Commons, and hundreds of representatives on local authorities. Finally, there is a Publications Department issuing books, pamphlets, posters and novelties, and responsible for the numerous "house" journals of coöperative organizations. Related to these departments are Trade Associations, bringing coöperative officials and committeemen into contact with the technical as well as the legislative aspects of the coal trade, the milk trade and the drug trade—associations which pool the Movement's experience and capacities for advancing trade as well as for defending trade interests. There is also a Joint-Propaganda Committee of the Union and the C.W.S. undertaking spade work in areas where Coöperation is weak, promoting annual Trades and Business Conferences and superintending a National Propaganda Campaign which has been since 1927 a vital element in coöperative progress.

As we have seen, the work of the Union and of several of its departments is conducted through sectional boards. On the one hand, contact with individual societies is sustained by further subdivision of the sections into district associations. On the other hand, the elected members of the sectional board comprise a Central Board. This Central Board appoints the Union's representatives to its own departmental committees, other representatives being the nominees of the appropriate national federations and auxiliary federations. The C.W.S., the S.C.W.S., the Coöperative Productive Federation and the Coöperative party, for example, are represented on the Joint-Parliamentary Committee; the Women's Coöperative Guild, the National Coöperative Men's Guild, the National Guild of Coöperators (an association of men and women) and the British Federation of Coöperative Youth play a part in the National Educational Council controlling the Education Department, and so on. The Central Board also appoints the Executive Committee of the Coöperative Union, controlling the work of all the departments and committees of the Union. This Executive Committee and representatives of the C.W.S., the S.C.W.S., the Coöperative party, the Coöperative Productive Federation and the Coöperative Press constitute the National Coöperative Authority, unifying leadership and making every section of a diverse movement responsive to a national mind.

Congress, the greatest event in the coöperative calendar, is the authority from which the Central Board derives its power. This Coöperative Congress meets in each sectional area in turn, the selection of its president, the rarest honor in the gift of British Coöperation, being intrusted to coöperative organizations in the section. As many as 2,000 delegates gather on the Monday morning of Whitweek to go through the four hundred pages of the Central Board's report, review every aspect of Coöperation at work, and take part in the special conferences of auxiliary agencies which are now a feature of Congress. Congress deliberates for three or four days. It is quite likely to spend as much time on a problem of amalgamation between two small retail societies as on matters affecting world trade and world peace. It has all the weaknesses of its size. Occasionally its proceedings are marked by rich comedy. A year or two back it protested unanimously against a decision of the British Broadcasting Corporation not to broadcast the president's speech and, when that august person had been on his feet for only ten minutes, had to be restrained from resolving that the remainder of his speech be held as read! Yet Congress is impressive in its efficiency. Its oratory reaches a high level. It has considerable value in bringing coöperative ideas into consonance and in enabling local key men and women to mark out future leaders from among the delegates.

The net result of this plethora of coöperative organization is that a national voluntary movement is more integrated than any of its trade and political rivals. Thousands of agencies, meeting weekly, are discussing coöperative problems, informing an ever-widening circle of ordinary men and women about coöperative principles and practice, and offering to everyone opportunity for service to his fellows. So democracy is preserved and the Forgotten Man enters into possession of his kingdom.

At Congress for one week the trumpets sound and the flags of battle are flown. For fifty-two weeks the Coöperative Union Headquarter's staff and the hundreds and thousands of men and women responding to its leadership are linked with Coöperation's powerful organs of trade in the conduct of a campaign against the untruth, the injustice and the lack of economy in production and exchange to which coöperators attribute many of the evils of unemployment and poverty.

VII.

State, Trust and the Consumer

UNTIL recent years Great Britain was regarded as the spiritual home of Free Trade and the philosophic stronghold of economic individualism. An importer of raw materials, her soil was thought to be unpropitious for the growth of monopoly. "A nation of shopkeepers," she was believed to be opposed, unalterably, to Protection, the only possible "mother of the trust" in so individualistic a country.

This reputation was undeserved and, indeed, libelous. It was based upon the misconception that British Capitalism differs from American, German or any other Capitalism. It assumed that, watchful though the Briton was of his interest as a moneylender abroad, he had no eye on the main chance at home. The truth reveals the Briton as less quixotic and more practical. Neither his law nor his institution deify free competition. They sustain private ownership of wealth. The early nineteenth-century demand for freedom to compete destroyed the Mercantile System, but it did not deny the right of freedom to combine. Laissez faire was merely the political expression of desire for personal freedom to accumulate, to enjoy the profits of enterprise without let or hindrance. Over the last hundred years, legislature and law courts have been converting this desire for freedom to accumulate into an inalienable prerogative. Thus modern British Capitalism, responding to the need for maintaining profit upon price, passed from Free Trade to Protection with as little jar or friction as Dickens, surely the greatest representative of the English genius in literature, passed from humor to pathos; and no straining of the facts is involved in the statement that, in Great Britain today, the trust is the mother of the tariff.

In the same year when the Rochdale Pioneers began to organize the economic power of consumers, the first cartel in history reached its climax and saw the waning of its strength. This was the Newcastle Coal Vend. Beginning in the early years of the seventeenth century, the Newcastle Vend survived a royal proclamation revoking monopolies in 1609, survived antimonopoly acts of 1634 and 1636, and survived the dissolution of Parliament by Cromwell with its abrogation of royal favors. In 1720 and 1730, and again in 1738, the Vend defeated legislative attempts to release free merchants from its strangle hold, and in 1771 it emerged as the model upon which later Continental cartels were based. The coal-owners on Tyne and Wear, members of the Vend, fixed prices insuring profits to inferior collieries, allotted quotas, imposed fines upon those parties to the Vend who exceeded their production quotas or undercut prices, and "dumped" coal abroad in order to sustain its scarcity value at home. They operated in collaboration with coal factors who formed a ring round London, then the most important coal market in the country. They promoted Parliamentary bills to prevent the expansion of the railway system, a dangerous rival to the system of transport by sea which they controlled. Individually, they inflated their capital and equipped their pits with excessive plant in order to establish claims for higher quotas in a growing market, the economic burdens thus imposed on the industry being passed on to the consumer in retail prices. But the Vend failed to face the problem implicit in all forms of organization for promoting private interest—the problem of individual rapacity. When competition from rival coal fields threatened to break prices in London in 1844, members declined to reduce output and refused to pay fines, amounting to £49,790, to compensate colleagues damaged by the excess of output. So died the Vend. But in other commodities the cartel persisted. It persisted in exploiting "the man on the Clapham omnibus" for eighty-four years, then was accorded full legal status by him, "the reasonable man," who is invoked by His Majesty's Judges when creating new precedents. Until 1928 members of a cartel were treated, legally, as members of a trade union. Their combination was not regarded as contrary to the public good, but the courts knew nothing of and did not recognize their "gentlemen's agreement." A man could break the agreement, just as a trade unionist can blackleg on his fellows. A cartel could fine the recalcitrant member just as a trade union can fine a blackleg. If, however, the cartel breaker or the blackleg refused to submit to arbitrary penalties, no court would insist that he swallow his medicine. Thus the court merely redeemed the cartel from illegality without giving sanction to the methods by which it maintained its power. The anomalies of this position were ended in 1928 when the Court of Appeal, second only to the House of Lords as the voice of authority in the British Judiciary, reversed a decision of a lower court in the case of the *English Hop Growers* v. *Dering*. The plaintiff society was an amalgamation of hop growers organized to control the output and regulate the price of hops. Dering, a member of the society, agreed to produce only the quota of hops allotted to him, to deliver the hops when grown to the society's representatives for sale, and to refrain from their disposal through any other agent. Dering deliberately broke his agreement and, when sued, challenged its legality. The Court of Appeal decided unanimously in favor of the society. Giving judgment, Lord Justice Scrutton stated the opinion of the modern "reasonable man" in terms which would have shocked the eminently reasonable Adam Smith. "In view of the fluctuating character of the yearly supply of hops," he said, "I see nothing unreasonable in hop growers combining to secure a steady and profitable price by eliminating competition amongst themselves and putting the marketing in the hands of one agent, with full power to fix prices and hold up supplies, the benefit and loss being divided amongst the members."[1]

The persistent endeavor of the courts today is to evolve,

1. C. H. S. Fifoot, M.A., *English Law and Its Background*, p. 211.

for the satisfaction of private commercial interests, some doctrine in the law of contract analogous to the law which secures
landlords in their monopoly. We may illustrate the point by
glancing at the legal history of Leicester Square and its garden, situated within a stone's throw of Piccadilly, London,
"the center of the world." The owner of the garden, a man
named Tulk, sold it to one Elms, on condition that it was not
built upon. The aim of this stipulation, presumably, was to
preserve the amenities of a sanctuary for bird life and love
and, incidentally, improve the site value of the surrounding
land. Elms sold the gardens to another man, Moxhay, who
was no party to the agreement between Elms and Tulk. But
Tulk in 1848 secured an injunction restraining Moxhay from
infringing the Tulk-Elms contract. The court sustained the
injunction. It held that the restrictive covenant runs with
land, however often ownership of the land may change.[2] And
the obvious tendency of the law today is toward granting the
twentieth-century manufacturer the privilege it conferred
upon the nineteenth-century landowner, a privilege that is
without precedent since a covenant or contract does not run
with goods. Tom may sell to Dick and make it a condition of
sale that Dick will not retail the goods at less than a fixed
price. If Dick disposes of the goods to Harry and Harry re-
tails at less than the fixed price, Tom has no redress against
Harry, who is not privy to the contract between Tom and
Dick. This position is unsatisfactory to the price fixer under
modern business conditions in which a complex organization
has been interposed between manufacturer and consumer. The
price fixer pays his own private detective agency to check up
on retailers who cut prices. He refuses to supply and endeav-
ors to bankrupt retailers who interfere with his monopoly.
He requires the force of law behind this bullying and brow-
beating if he is to exploit consumers effectively. Yet the law
is strange in this case: while the Court of Appeal upholds

2. *Idem*, p. 233.

such punitive action as the imposition of fines and the application of a "stop list" to unruly retailers, the Court of Criminal Appeal has described the threat to withhold supplies unless a fine is paid as demanding money with menaces and a punishable offense! Whatever the fate of the consumer, hope need not die in the hearts of the monopolists. It is a fact of history that when the action of any great vested interest is in breach of law, the British Parliament and the British courts change the law. Already the Agricultural Marketing Acts endow producers with power to fix prices and punish retailers who offend against their regulations. These Acts are "Commodity Inclosure Acts" backed by the same authority that was put behind the Land Inclosure Act one hundred and thirty-five years ago. The *fait accompli*, like possession, is more than nine tenths of law. It is law.

From the days of the decline of the Newcastle Vend, amalgamation and combination have made giant strides in Great Britain. Their progress has been by way of cartels for price fixing, then on to that close association of trades engaged in similar processes called horizontal organization, culminating in the price-fixing horizontal trust developing vertically to secure control of the sources of raw material and perfection of unity on behalf of private profit making.

Consider the soap combine, to which only the Coöperative Movement offers any real opposition. As long ago as 1867 soap was subject to price fixing. In 1886, the firm of Lever Brothers, Ltd., entered the industry and immediately began a process of amalgamation which would have been brought to a climax in 1906, but for a surprising outburst of public opposition. Lever proposed a fusion of ten of the principal manufacturers and then, in some mysterious way, fell foul of the *Daily Mail*, founded in 1896 as the first halfpenny daily newspaper and commanding in 1906 a sale in excess of 750,-000 copies daily. Some observers take the view that Lever refused to advertise in the *Daily Mail* and that its proprietor determined to hit back. Others suggest that the *Mail's* attack was nothing more or less than a stunt, designed to make people talk and to get circulation. In the event, the newspaper exposed the soap trust plan, alleged, wrongfully, that short weight was a trick of the soapmakers' trade, and paid £250,000 to settle the resulting legal actions out of court. The publicity given the trust plan, however, roused the nation. Lever announced that the fusion was "absolutely and finally dissolved" and proceeded, quietly and unobtrusively, to secure by absorption what it had failed to obtain by fusion. Within five years all the undertakings in the abandoned merger had been acquired, together with control of about thirty firms in France, Belgium, Germany, Switzerland, America, Japan, Australia, Canada and Africa. By 1913 the original authorized capital of £1,500,000 had leaped to £30,-000,000. By the end of the Great War, authorized capital stood at £100,000,000. Today it is £130,000,000, and soap is only one of many commodities purveyed by Unilever, Ltd., with a domain ranging from Walls's sausage counters in English village shops to the Great Wall of China.

Lever controls 80 per cent of Great Britain's soap trade. In association with the Margarine Union, it dominates the margarine trade. Through the Home and Colonial, Ltd., it operates 5,500 chain stores with 40,000 employees, these stores being labeled Lipton's, Maypole Dairies, Meadow Dairies, Pearks Dairies, and so on. Until recently, a director of this Lever-controlled distributive grocery trust occupied a seat on the directorate of London Express Newspapers, Ltd., owners of the *Daily Express* which, inspired by Lord Beaverbrook, is a sleepless opponent of the Coöperative Movement. According to the chairman's speech at the 1936 meeting of Unilever, there are few parts of the world where the combine has not its own factories and selling points, so that it can "expect to find compensation in one country for adverse conditions in another." It owns two fleets of trawlers supplying its retail fish shops. It owns ship repair and construction yards for the building and upkeep of river fleets, canneries for fish and vegetable products, ice cream plants, a silk factory and a weaving mill, "to mention some at random." It looms large in the real estate business.

What has been the effect on the consumer of trustification in the soap trade? Has it led to economy of production?

In 1924 the late Lord Leverhulme explained that all the soap subsidiaries in the combine were in competition as "the only way the string of the bow was kept tight." He verified the view formed by the subcommittee on the Soap Industry of the Committee on Trusts, which reported in 1920 that "although the acquired companies have the benefit of Lever Brothers' experts and of their laboratories, they . . . have effected little or no economy in any of the items which go to make up the cost of the manufacture of soap."[3] It is doubtful if internal competition does, in fact, keep the string of the bow tight. Overhead charges incurred in selling are as likely to be high where competition is nominal as where it is real. Under such circumstances the job of the commercial traveler is not to sell the product of his company. It is to induce in the immediate buyer a willingness to continue to accept the dictation of the combine. Since the price of dictation is not paid by that buyer but by the ultimate consumer, inducement may too easily take the form of an invitation to collaborate in exploiting the consumer. That is a beckoning condition toward excessive price fixing. Moreover, the Lever method at that time, as the Committee on Trusts noted, was debited with many of the evils of the cartel but could be credited with the economies effected by real concentration of the manufacturing and selling process, for "the prices fixed by the Association [i.e., The United Kingdom Soap Manufacturers' Association, controlled by Lever Brothers] will usually be such as to afford to the least efficient member of the Association a sufficient profit." Indeed, the Committee declared that "the evidence does not satisfy us that these economies have been substantial, or represent to the public any advantage comparable with the

3. Command Paper 1126, p. 13.

loss and danger involved to them in the fixing of excessive prices." The Committee uncovered this danger to the public as actual and urgent. Between February and April, 1920, it pointed out, the cost of raw materials fell about £15 per ton, and the retail price of soap declined by 1*d*. per pound. Between April and December, the cost of raw materials fell again by over £32 per ton, but the retail price was not reduced. Soap which should have been charged at not more than 8½*d*. or 9*d*. per pound was being charged at 11*d*. per pound. Lord Leverhulme, giving evidence, was pleasingly frank with the Committee. He told them that, on a rising market, prices were based on replacement costs rather than on the cost of the materials used, lest his firms be flooded out with retailers' orders they could not meet! On a falling market, prices were based on the cost of the materials used, because, explained his lordship naïvely, the bulk of profits made at the high level were not available to offset losses (*sic*) at the low level, since they had been absorbed by the Excess Profits Duty then imposed by the Government. In the effort to relieve trust shareholders of the charge that they were "having it both ways," his lordship forgot that the Finance Act allowed losses for reduced profits to be set against earlier excess profits.

As late as 1926, an economist of repute, reviewing the profits of Lever Brothers and thirteen allied companies, remarked that "they do not appear to have yielded an unreasonably high return on invested capital."[4] In 1913 profits on home sales were 10.93 per cent. In 1918 they were 16.23 per cent—an increase of 86 per cent although there had been no increase in output. In addition there had been considerable dilution of capital. In 1919 Lever paid £4,000,000 for the ordinary shares of two companies with a nominal original value of £900,000. A few months later the trust paid a premium of 550 per cent for the 1,227,165 one-pound ordinary[5]

4. P. Fitzgerald, *Industrial Combination*, p. 71.
5. i.e., common.

shares of the Niger Company, Ltd., the price being £6 10s. per share, although the Stock Exchange valuation for the preceding six months averaged about £4. Within the next four weeks one-pound deferred[6] shares in yet another company were purchased at £13 10s., and the ordinary shares were guaranteed a dividend twice as high as that paid in the most prosperous year of the acquired company's history. Frequent issues of bonus shares lowered the nominal and concealed the real rate of profit.

The only guardian of the consumer against the dangers here revealed is the Coöperative Movement. Over the period investigated by the Committee on Trusts, the best coöperative household soap was sold at prices lower than those charged by the members of The United Kingdom Soap Manufacturers' Association by sums ranging from £2 10s. to £26 per ton. The Committee also commented on the coöperative practice of following the raw material market: "The Coöperative Wholesale Society's prices have, on a rising market, been based (broadly) on actual costs and on a falling market on replacement costs. The Coöperative Wholesale Society have generally taken the lower of the two costs which . . . is the exact reverse of what other soap makers have done." To that proof of the economy of Coöperation we need only add that, in 1930, coöperative production represented 15 per cent of the total weight of soap manufactured in Great Britain (1,400,000 cwts., out of 9,200,000 cwts.) and 9 per cent of the total wholesale price (£3,000,000 out of £32,000,000).

It would be wrong to imagine that the development of trusts with potentially antisocial tendencies is unusual in Great Britain. When, in 1916, the British Government decided that if the resources of Great Britain were left to the care of private enterprise the Great War might be lost, the newly formed Ministry of Munitions found that almost every industry it approached was trustified; and to what effect was indicated in the statement made by Mr. David Lloyd George

6. i.e., preferred.

(House of Commons, August 18, 1919) that the costing system of the Ministry reduced prices charged for raw materials by £440,000,000 from the date of the Ministry's formation until November, 1918. Between 1914 and 1917, retail prices rose at the nearly uniform rate of 23 per cent per annum. The Ministry of Food fixed prices to yield a round 10 per cent on capital, and for two years they remained stable at about 110 over prewar. As soon as supplies were decontrolled, a rise at the rate of 23 per cent per annum was resumed in response to the demand for profit from shareholders of diluted or watered stock. So capital began to fall more certainly into its two present-day categories. There was industrial capital, necessary for the purchase of plant and the organization of the market. And there was finance capital, the increment of monetary manipulation, the interest on which represented the fresh colossal burdens on enterprise arising from monopoly. Capital which, in the early years of the industrial era, sat heavily upon the back of the worker, had now invaded his pocket. Exploitation of the consumer alone could secure it in its gross profits.

Suggestions of a speculative shortage of wheat in 1924 sent the price of flour soaring and focused public attention on the milling industry. It was found that, whereas fifty years before there were 10,000 corn mills, the bulk of the trade had passed into the hands of three mighty businesses. Two of these firms were Spillers, Ltd., which now has an authorized capital of £5,200,000, and Ranks, Ltd., now a £7,295,-000 company. The third firm was the C.W.S., an effective barrier to complete private control. In 1930 the flour output of the C.W.S. amounted to 17 per cent of the total weight of national output (650,000 tons in 3,800,000 tons) and 15 per cent of the total wholesale value (£10,000,000 out of £67,000,000). An attempt to assess the relative efficiency of various types of mills was made in 1925 by the Royal Commission on Food Prices. It found that on flour milled by the Coöperative Movement and associated companies (the combine) net profit was 1s. 2d. per sack compared with 7d. for port mills and 10½d. for town and country mills, and it reported: "Although we are not at liberty to give separately the figures for the co-operative societies, it may be stated that their margins of profit were higher than those disclosed by the average for the group. It must be remembered, however, that a proportion of the profits is returned to their members in the form of dividend. In this connection we agree with the view taken by the Linlithgow Committee . . . that the comparatively satisfactory position of the co-operative societies' mills is probably due to their having suffered less severely than other mills from the expansion of milling capacity and subsequent short-time working, and to the fact that with a more or less assured outlet for their produce they are under no necessity to maintain costly selling agencies. The actual figures show that a saving is effected in overhead charges."[7]

Whence came the threat to the housewife, a penny on whose quartern loaf raised the nation's bread bill by £10,-000,000 a year? It came from local associations of master bakers who fixed prices, obtained the aid of millers in boycotting bakers who cut prices and, in the words of the Linlithgow Committee, used "coercive and dictatorial methods which are not only reprehensible in themselves but are clearly detrimental to the public interest." Standing against these local "rings" and frequently breaking them were the bakeries owned by retail coöperative societies. These bakeries obtained a yield of between 93 and 95 quartern loaves per 280-pound sack of flour, compared with the general private trade average of 92 quartern loaves. Although trade union conditions prevailed in coöperative bakeries, their labor costs averaged 5s. 3½d. per sack against the overall average of 6s. ¾d., "the difference," said the Food Commission, "being probably due to the fact that their production is on a rather larger scale, and certain economies in labour are practicable which the smaller private bakeries cannot effect."[8] On evidence which,

7. Command Paper 2390, p. 57.   8. Command Paper 2390, p. 35.

Sun Flour Mills, Manchester. The largest single milling unit in Europe although meager, may be conclusive, coöperative distribution costs were put at 8*s.* 9¼*d.* per sack against an average of 9*s.* 6*d.* for private bakers. In the result, the average net profit of fifteen private retail firms which sent in accounts was 6.1 per cent against 10.5 per cent for a similar number of coöperative societies whose accounts were comparable. Thus the coöperative societies "while selling bread of a quality which is claimed as being up to the average at no more, and in some cases less, than the ruling price, were able to return about 2/– in the £ to members on purchases." One of many examples of low coöperative prices was offered by the Royal Arsenal Coöperative Society, which showed that from 1920 until 1924, while *Labour Gazette* bread figures varied from 1*s.* 4*d.* to 8½*d.* per quartern loaf, the price to that Society's members varied from 1*s.* 3*d.* to 8*d.*; and during 1924, when the *Labour Gazette* figure was 8½*d.* the actual cost to Woolwich consumers (inclusive of the dividend on purchases) was 7½*d.* The Food Commission concluded that "as a rule there cannot be an advance in bread without the consent of the co-operative society," and "the loss to the public from price fixing arrangements in the baking trade is not likely to be serious in those districts where the co-operative societies pursue an independent policy directed toward keeping bread prices as low as possible."

The milk situation in England may be explained in terms of statistics although it is difficult to understand in terms of common sense. All supplies are controlled by a Milk Marketing Board enjoying statutory powers to license producers, fix prices, subsidize the manufacture of milk surplus to the requirements of the liquid market, and itself enter into possession of creameries and manufacturing plants. During 1935 the Board imposed penalties amounting to £7,461 upon 316 registered producers, fifteen of these penalties being imposed for selling milk at less than the prescribed retail price.

The first aim of the Board is to insure profitable returns to farmers. It strives also to improve the quality of herds and to increase liquid consumption by various forms of publicity and by selling milk to children in schools at reduced rates. In the milk year 1933–34 the Board handled 845,000,000 gallons of milk of which 634,000,000 were absorbed by the liquid market and 211,000,000—so-called "surplus" milk— went to manufacture. In 1934–35 the Board handled 981,-000,000 gallons, of which 665,000,000 gallons, including nearly 23,000,000 gallons sold under the milk-in-schools scheme, were absorbed by the liquid market, and 316,000,-000 gallons went to manufacture. Clearly, the Board has failed to liquidate the surplus milk problem, although it has "solved" the farmers' problem. This it has done by paying farmers an average price of 1s. 3½d. per gallon for all milk and selling the surplus to manufacturers at prices ranging from 4½d. to 7½d. per gallon. Thus every two gallons of milk drunk by the consumer carries a price toll, rising from 8d. to 11d., in respect of one gallon of milk used in manufacture. Reporting in November, 1936, a Milk Reorganization Commission suggested, *inter alia*, that the subsidy provided by the consumer amounted to about £5,000,000 per annum, in addition to which there is the cost of the administration of the Board itself. These figures do not include State subsidies paid by taxpaying consumers in aid of the Board's "stimulation of consumption" efforts and amounting to £1,500,000 up to September 30, 1937; nor do they include subsidies, in excess of £1,000,000 a year, to cover manufacturing losses. The position is not made less ludicrous by the fact that while the liquid milk market is almost immune from foreign competition, 5 per cent of the surplus milk is converted into condensed milk for export at a cost to the Exchequer of nearly £50,000 a year. Retail prices are so high that the public cannot afford to buy milk, so the country exports its product as condensed milk with a gift of public money in every tin!

The per capita consumption of milk in Great Britain is almost the lowest in Europe. Distributors, however, enjoy two compensations. Retail prices range with the highest in Europe and retail margins are protected against undercutting. Thus the Milk Marketing Board has enriched the ground for the growth of distributive combines.

Fortunately, the existence of fixed prices has not escaped the notice of consumers to whom the coöperative dividend on milk purchases now appears in its true light as a tangible, economic saving. Since 1912, when a Scottish society laid down one of the first pasteurizing plants in Great Britain, coöperative societies have been advancing steadily in the dairy business. They have built up a reputation as pioneers of a pure milk supply and established themselves in public esteem. Today, the trend of the milk trade is so strongly toward the coöperative store that the Milk Board permits private retailers to cut prices to an amount equal to the coöperative dividend! In 1934–35, the Coöperative Movement distributed 154,000,000 gallons (upward of 120,000,-000 gallons being pasteurized and bottled) or 22 per cent of the nation's liquid supplies. Every gallon paid the consumer a "divi" averaging 10 per cent. In the three years' life of the Milk Board, output, on the basis of a guaranteed price to farmers, increased by 14 per cent. In the same period coöperative trade on the basis of fixed retail prices, less a dividend averaging one halfpenny per quart, has increased 21 per cent.

Tea provides an excellent sample of a commodity which, difficult to monopolize at the source, may still be the subject of market rigging at the expense of consumers. The English and Scottish Joint C.W.S. is the world's largest distributor of tea and, with a turnover of 80,000,000 pounds a year, handles one fifth of the supplies poured into Mrs. Britain's teapot. In addition it sells 50,000,000 pounds a year overseas. Crops from its own estates in India and Ceylon meet less than one half of one month's trade and the Federation must resort to the Tea Exchange at Mincing Lane. There it exercises a restraining influence upon rings and riggers, frequently entering into battle with them on behalf of the consumer. One such battle roused the country in 1924 when, although a Labor Chancellor reduced the duty on tea by fourpence per pound, prices rose sharply. Private brokers had combined to negotiate the purchase of tea still unharvested, keep it off the market and hold dealers to ransom. In order to obtain forward purchases, they had to persuade growers that the market was breaking. Stocks were unloaded and prices fell. Contracts worth millions of pounds sterling were made on future harvests. Then came the Budget relief and a further price fall. The riggers were short of supplies. Market demand rose. Public demand rose. Prices were inflated until the whole Budget concession was filched from every consumer except the coöperative consumer. His tea organization bought heavily in a falling market. During the whole period of rising prices, it bought on the average only one fourth of its normal requirements. Thus it was enabled for four months to stabilize prices without varying the quality of its tea and to effect to coöperative customers a saving of £400,000—an immediate bonus in addition to the deferred dividend on purchases.

The E. and S.C.W.S. has exercised even more influence as a distributor. Long before 1918 it protested publicly against the practice of including the weight of the packet in the weight of tea sold over the counters of retail shops. This square-deal policy cost coöperators £90,000 a year; but it helped to force the passage in 1922 of a Sale-of-Tea-by-Net-Weight Act which brought all other traders into line and realized for all consumers a saving estimated now at £5,000,000 a year.

Look now at insurance, a vital social service and one in which, except through the Coöperative Insurance Society, the voice of the insured, the consumer, is still unheard. Despite the high-powered publicity of private companies, directed by 100,000 agents, and State provision of pensions to widows and orphans "the average husband and father of the British industrial class is certainly much under insured."[9] Even among the taxpaying class the amount of life insurance is equivalent to less than one year's income. The average life insurance per head of the whole population of England is only £55 compared with £190 in the U.S.A. As in other countries, the overwhelming volume of insurance income is industrial insurance; it is organized on a system of weekly house-to-house collection of the pennies of the working classes. In 1933 there were 87,000,000 policies for sums totaling £1,400,000,000. Of these, 66,000,000 policies for sums totaling £1,085,000 were in the hands of fifteen companies. The tariffs and benefits of these companies, in the main, are uniform. They operate agreements covering so many sections of the business that competition, while it exists and, in fact, is feverish in restricted fields, is reduced to a minimum. The Board of Trade requires a deposit of £15,000 from every company engaging in insurance. To a new company industrial business, the most profitable section of insurance, can be obtained only at a huge capital cost. In practice the new company can fight for business only on a restricted front, and there only under adverse conditions. It must offer terms that are more attractive than those already available. Unlike existing companies, it cannot subsidize, say, its motor business, at the expense of industrial policyholders. Insurance is virtually a monopoly; and a monopoly which makes the industrial policyholder the victim of every evil inherent in private enterprise.

Twenty-five years ago, a critic estimated that the poor industrial policyholder drew from insurance £1 for every £3 he paid as premium, and that the rich ordinary policyholder drew £4 for every £7 he paid as premium. By 1920

9. Report of Committee on Industrial Assurance presided over by Sir Benjamin Cohen, 1933, referred to hereafter as the Cohen Report. Command Paper 4376.

the position had improved somewhat. An official report[10] revealed that 44 per cent of the total premium income on industrial policies was absorbed by expenses and profits, so that of every shilling paid in premiums sixpence three farthings were returned to the insured in benefits. That criticism proved to be salutary. In the course of thirteen years the companies reduced expenses to 38.3 per cent. Even on the basis of existing methods, however, the Cohen Report described 30 per cent as a desirable maximum.

The social results of high-pressure salesmanship, more insistent upon securing business than upon serving consumers, may be seen in the number of lapsed policies. In 1929 nearly 10,000,000 policies were issued. Of these more than 6,000,000 were discontinued. Since premiums had been paid for periods up to two years on 1,250,000 policies, free policies were issued or surrender values granted. Thus 4,750,-000,000 lapsed. The insurance coverage of those who had taken out policies which lapsed within a short time amounted in value to one fifth of the premium income they had paid. In fourteen years, declared a speaker in the House of Commons on March 29, 1934, there had been 100,000,000 lapsed policies involving the public in a loss of £100,000,-000. Over that period the income of the companies was £772,000,000, of which management expenses and shareholders' profits took £315,000,000 and policyholders £272,-000,000.

Now, quite apart from the relief from income tax allowed on insurance payments to a comparatively small section of the community, the whole of this gigantic business has been built into the fabric of the State by legislation. National Health Insurance Acts make insurance, operated by companies and societies "approved" by the Board of Trade, compulsory for nearly 16,000,000 workers; they have

10. Report of the Board of Trade Industrial Assurance Committee, presided over by Lord Parmoor, in 1920, referred to hereafter as the Parmoor Report. Command Paper 614.

erected one of the several hothouses in which the plant of private insurance can flourish. Workmen's Compensation Acts inforce employer's liability although they do not make insurance by the employer compulsory. The result is that a workman claiming compensation for an industrial accident against a small employer may find the defendant going bankrupt to evade payment. If the worker sues an insured employer, he must do battle with the array of legal talent available to a wealthy institution. Unless the workman is supported by his trade union, he is likely to accept an unfair settlement rather than face the costly litigation involved in carrying his case through an inferior court to the Court of Appeal and, perhaps, on to the House of Lords. His one protection lies with the judge, who must approve every settlement in conformity with a law awarding the widow of an employee killed at work the paltry maximum sum of £300 for herself and £600 for herself and all dependent children. Of every £100 contributed by employers to cover workmen's liability it is estimated that £48 goes to the relief of the victims of industrial accidents and £52 goes to the insurance companies and the legal profession. Of a different order is compulsory third-party motor insurance, enacted in 1930 and bringing much grist to the insurance mill. Every motorist must provide against claims by injured pedestrians. Let us follow an injured party through the court. He finds that the real defendent is an insurance company enlisting the aid of skilled counsel and expert medical witnesses. It is open to the company to plead that its client, the motorist, did not disclose essential particulars, such as his record of previous accidents and convictions, when the insurance was effected, and to repudiate liability on that account. Thus the law permits the company to charge premiums to a client whose bona fides it has no responsibility for investigating, to pocket these premiums and to evade all liabilities deriving from them; and the pedestrian can be ruined financially and denied compensation by legal costs, even if he establishes his case against the motorist. It is not surprising that this loophole has been exploited by mushroom companies which have issued attractive prospectuses to motorists, taken their premiums, piled up enormous liabilities backed by microscopical assets, then gone bankrupt, leaving their clients uninsured and third parties without compensation. What is surprising is this; the State has left third-party insurance to exploitation by private companies; the Board of Trade, which has power to investigate insurance finances, has been consistent in taking action only after companies have become hopelessly insolvent. Numerous recommendations to end these scandals, made by important Government committees, have been ignored. Indeed, apart from the creation of the office of Industrial Assurance Commissioner, to which the policyholder may appeal, legislation on insurance has taken the form of a series of acts of indemnity. Companies, in the words of the Cohen Report, have disregarded "the law in so far as it has proved inconvenient to them." They have presented Parliament with a *fait accompli*. Parliament, obediently, has changed the law the companies were breaking by legalizing practices in breach of law.

The fortunes of the Prudential Assurance Company, Ltd., with a paid-up capital of £1,450,000, 20,000 employees in Great Britain and £780,000,000 of policies, and a business whose reputation for efficiency and probity is unchallengeable, offer a rough guide to where insurance income goes.

About ninety years ago, groups of people, largely under the inspiration of Rochdale Coöperation, formed mutual associations to provide themselves with death benefits and similar services. One of these groups was the Prudential Mutual Assurance Investment and Loan Association. By 1860 it had a nominal capital of £100,000 held by a tiny number of shareholders. In 1886 the nominal capital stood at £1,000,000, the whole of which, except for an original sum of £10,000 subscribed in hard cash, seemed by 1920 to have been "handed over to the shareholders in the shape of bonus." How capital accumulation has been achieved is suggested by an analysis of the division of profits. In the industrial section, after payments to reserve funds, £360,000 free of income tax goes to "A" shareholders. Of the remainder, policyholders take three fourths, the "A" shareholders an eighth, and "such of the outdoor staff as the directors shall determine" the final eighth. In the ordinary section, after contributions to a contingency fund, holders of profit-sharing policies take nine tenths, the remaining tenth, subject to provision for a special contingency reserve fund, going to the "A" shareholders. In the general section, the directors have discretion to give such profits as they think fit to policyholders and staff, the remainder being divided between "A" shareholders and "B" shareholders, in the proportions of one quarter and three quarters. In 1935 a surplus of £9,100,000 was realized in the industrial and ordinary sections. Policyholders were allocated £6,500,000 or 1 per cent on the total value of policies then outstanding, and "A" shareholders £1,175,000 or 92 per cent on their capital holdings. In the three years up to 1935, bonuses to policyholders aggregated about 4 per cent on the average annual value of policies. Profits to "A" shareholders aggregated 278 per cent.[11]

"In 1930," according to the Cohen Report, "practically the whole of the minimum dividend of 50 per cent (free of tax) on £250,000 of new capital which had been raised in 1929 was charged upon the surplus of the industrial assurance fund, although the new capital had no connection with and served no purpose of the company's industrial assurance business and although, further, the interest earning of the £1,000,000 premium at which the new capital was raised was paid into a reserve account from which equally the industrial assurance business derived no benefit."

Unlike the Bank of England, the Prudential does not create credit. Like the Bank of England, it controls the flow

11. Labor Research Department, *The Prudential and Its Money*, p. 16.

of investment and, with assets exceeding £300,000,000, is an important nerve center of enterprise. It has money links and directorate connections with banks at home and abroad and with other insurance companies. It is a large investor in a time-payment furniture firm, in national newspapers (The News of the World, Ltd., and Sunday Pictorial Newspapers, Ltd.,) and in the State subsidized beet sugar business. It dominates the share lists of Marks and Spencer, the famous maximum price store. In short, insurance, whether operated by the Prudential or any other company, wields an influence on social and economic life transcending any possibility visualized by the consumer paying his small weekly contribution in return for a not too generous service.

Late in starting, the Coöperative Insurance Society is today the fastest growing insurance institution in Great Britain. Until 1918, when it took over the Planet Friendly Assurance Collecting Society, its business was concerned mainly with the special requirements of coöperative societies for fire, fidelity, and similar forms of coverage. Not until 1886, nineteen years after the Society was formed, did coöperators contemplate entry into life insurance. They looked with disfavor upon a system which was so costly in its administration as to be contrary to an essential precept of coöperative practice—that the consumer should spend his income in the most economical way. First ventures in life insurance spurned the method of house-to-house collection of premiums, and sought to sell insurance over the store counter. A community habituated to house-to-house collection and still unaware of its lack of economy did not respond, and coöperators were obliged to explore other avenues of development. By 1904 a scheme of collective insurance was introduced, based on a charge of one penny per pound on the sales of retail societies, and guaranteeing to dependents of deceased members benefits in proportion to their average purchases in the three years preceding death.[12] The scheme met with immediate

12. See Chapter V.

success. Administration costs were limited to 3 per cent. A new principle in insurance, which has been applied more extensively in America than in Great Britain, was pursued vigorously. Today, the C.I.S. owned by the C.W.S. and the S.C.W.S. and, with a nominal capital of £100,000 (20 per cent called up), engages in every type of insurance. Between 1915 and 1935 its premium income in all classes of business expanded from £309,000 to nearly £7,000,000, annual claims paid rose from £186,000 to over £2,000,000, assets grew from £683,000 to £21,750,000 and its army of full-time agents increased from 75 to 5,000.[13] The Society now holds sixth place among companies doing industrial business, fifteenth place in ordinary life business and, in new motor business obtained, first place. Its surpluses, after payment of interest on capital at the fixed rate of 5 per cent, are devoted mainly to adding to the sums recoverable by policy-holders. The cumulative effect of expansion with economy in administration must make the C.I.S. a formidable competitor of private companies within the next few years. Even in its young manhood, it was able to offer £12 10s. insurance for a penny a week, while other companies were giving only £10 10s. Its 5,000 agents are propagandists for the coöperative stores in the districts they canvass. Frequently they enjoy the use of lists of members of retail societies. Their approach is to a good type of citizen so well-disposed toward coöperative enterprise that insurance business need not be forced. Thus losses to the public through lapsed policies are reduced. In the C.I.S. industrial section in 1935 surrenders amounted to only £199,000 in a total business of £3,732,000.

Publicity, whether its task be sound or silence, is essential to monopoly in a political democracy. This duty in modern Britain is assigned to the Press.

Twenty years ago, in support of his advocacy of nonnationalization of the mines, the late Lord Rhondda added newspapers to the trade in coal, beer, textiles, transport, insurance

13. Baron, *Coöperative Insurance*, p. 143 *et seq.*

and patent medicines being conducted by the Cambrian Coal Combine. The newspaper chain Lord Rhondda founded persists in the Berry group, with Lord Camrose at its head. This group controls two national daily newspapers, three national Sunday newspapers, a score of provincial morning, evening and weekly newspapers and about one hundred weekly and monthly magazines. Next in size is the Rothermere group, owning two national dailies, two Sunday newspapers, one evening and a number of provincial evenings, followed by the Beaverbrook group with one daily, one Sunday newspaper and one evening. When the Rothermere-Beaverbrook groups are not exchanging shares in each other's property, they are engaging in joint promotion of separate journals. The "Cocoa Press," dominated by the firm of Cadbury, produce a national daily, the most distinctively "Left" newspaper in Great Britain and a London evening paper. Then there is Odhams Press, Ltd., an enterprising firm of printers with a great Sunday newspaper, a popular weekly and numerous magazines and trade journals. Odhams hold 51 per cent of the share capital and control editorial conduct of the *Daily Herald*, the official organ of the Labor party which, through the Trades Union Congress, holds 49 per cent of the share capital and controls the editorial policy.

Newspapers ceased long ago to be tied by shareholdings and directorates to Big Business. They are tied by the necessity for obtaining advertising revenue, the source of which is the big store magnate, the manufacturer of branded, fixed-price goods and the producer of patent medicines.

The penny the public pays for its newspaper seldom covers the cost of newsprint alone. From advertising revenues come the funds which finance plant, news and editorial services, distribution and the handsome profits enjoyed by shareholders in a £100,000,000-trust industry. With few exceptions, newspapers are overcapitalized. To carry the ever-growing burdens of capital interest, more and more space has been devoted to advertisements in recent years. To secure these advertisements, newspapers have sought to attract readers by means of costly gambling contests and free gifts, and to bind them as registered readers through accident insurance schemes. The two most successful purveyors of nonnewspaper services wrapped in news sheets have between them a sale of nearly 4,500,000 copies daily. With two other papers, these "popular" dailies sell over 7,000,000 copies to a population of 11,000,000 families. Together, the four national "popular" dailies comprise the shopwindow of the mail-order side of Britain's big stores and are an essential part of the selling machinery of all commodities seeking a nationwide market. At the peak of the process of converting the Press from a large number of small circulation newspapers, selling news and opinion, to a small number of large circulation newspapers, selling soap and pills, the capital cost of daily circulation was estimated to be as high as 10s. a reader. Since advertisers were unwilling to divide existing appropriations among newspapers circulating fewer than 1,000,000 copies daily, the price of new journalistic enterprise was beyond the resources of all but Crœsus. And so it remains.

On its distributive side, newspaper organization takes the form of a cartel. The producing trusts, as a matter of policy, grant agencies only to small men. They themselves dare not undertake distribution lest a critical public realizes how gladly its Press has sacrificed freedom for servitude to wealth. But they can, and do, prevent the growth of a distributive combine strong enough to use the weapon of boycott to secure better terms for news agents. Thus the activities of news agents are directed toward zoning areas and licensing shops in order to prevent coöperative or any other form of enterprise entering the industry through distribution.

These circumstances presented the Coöperative Movement with a grave problem. A growing trade organization, affected by the trend of legislation not less than by the postwar drive toward monopoly, could ignore the existence of a hostile Press only at its peril. Inside the Coöperative Movement a special federation, the Coöperative Press, had established a number of "Movement" journals.[14] Nevertheless, leading coöperators regarded it as intolerable that opinion among the mass membership of coöperative societies should continue to be influenced by an anticoöperative Press.

Approach to the problem was slow and tentative. Coöperators, as we have seen, do not like to buy experience; they prefer to acquire it firsthand; and the record of Labor and trade union failure in Fleet Street was not encouraging. In 1929 an old Radical Sunday paper, *Reynolds News,* came onto the market. Nobody in Fleet Street had much confidence in its future for *Reynolds* had not kept pace with the times, either in plant or personnel. The Coöperative Press bought *Reynolds* and a new editorial policy took shape gradually. A circulation, based entirely on the paper's tradition and, consequently, likely to dissolve slowly, was stabilized. Then the way to win and register readers for *Reynolds* became clear. Other newspapers registered readers against accident. By expanding collective insurance schemes of coöperative societies, *Reynolds* could register the reader's dependents for benefit in the event of the reader's death. Three years of experience revealed that an actuarially sound insurance scheme could provide a bonus of $33\frac{1}{3}$ per cent to every coöperator registered with *Reynolds* and purchasing the paper for a minimum period of three months. Thus a male coöperator whose average purchases from a retail society entitled his wife to £30 on his death, could add £10 to that benefit by registering with the newspaper owned by the Coöperative Movement.

During those years, too, confidence was created that the giant's task coöperators had tackled was not beyond the bounds of achievement. Besides a newspaper, coöperators had boots and butter and furniture and a thousand other com-

14. *Coöperative News, Scottish Coöperator, Woman's Outlook, Our Circle* (for children), *The Millgate* (a monthly cultural journal), *The Citizen* (a monthly political and trade paper with localized editions). The C.W.S. publishes *The Producer* (monthly) and *The Wheatsheaf.*

modities to sell. Their newspaper could become their shop-window. So was evolved the idea of a coöperative collective advertising fund, to provide the essential revenue of a national coöperative newspaper and to finance an up-to-date Coöperative Press. This fund is fed by payments, on a three-yearly basis, of one farthing per pound of annual sales from retail societies and one eighth per pound of annual sales from federations supporting the scheme. It amounts now to £80,-000 a year. Out of the guarantees so provided, the C.W.S. Bank has financed the erection of an imposing newspaper building and the equipment of *Reynolds* with a plant which has put it in the forefront of Sunday journalism. *Reynolds* today is an intelligent paper with a popular appeal. As it has grown it has attracted attention from those private makers of good-class branded commodities who find part of their market in the Coöperative Movement. It is the only coöperative newspaper in the world commanding a sale through the ordinary channels of newspaper distribution; it is, indeed, the only coöperative commodity distributed through non-coöperative shops. Coöperation has broken the poverty barrier to democratic development in a difficult field for new enterprise.

Our examination of a cross section of British commerce, typical of all production and all services, justifies the thesis that the British consumer is in the grip of the trust and that it is to Coöperation, and not to the State, that the consumer must look meantime for protection and release. Numberless Government commissions and committees have exposed the dangers to the public inherent in the antisocial action of monopolies, the closing of one industrial field after another to new entrants, and the growing power of moneyed interests as dictators of the nation's economic destiny. Many of these commissions and committees have prescribed the remedy. Yet nothing has been done. The Press has been silent on matters of grave import. Successive governments, braving the charge that they are mere puppets of "the Invisible Empire of Big

Business," have ignored the remedies suggested by their own commissions and committees of inquiry, and have legalized spoliation of the people.

Nearly ten years ago 60 per cent of British industry was said to be outside the area of free competition. Great business houses, in the throes of rationalization, were put in pawn to the banks. The foundation of competing firms became increasingly costly and, if successful, a menace to the profits of their own as well as their opponents' shareholders. Take cigarette production as an example. Cigarette smoking is a habit stimulated by war. After every war from the Peninsular Campaign (1808–14) on, the cigarette gained more and more popularity over the pipe until 1907, when 26 per cent of the British tobacco trade was in cigarettes and 65 per cent in pipe tobacco. By the end of 1918, these figures were reversed, and it was their reversal that brought mechanization on a really gigantic scale to the industry. Mass production in one factory now requires command of a market for 15,000,-000 cigarettes a week. Command of such a market calls for extensive newspaper advertising and contact with hundreds of thousands of selling points. Capture of this mass market, while it would leave the profits of the Imperial Tobacco Company unimpaired, might well bankrupt every small man in the business without being profitable to the new entrant. As a result, economically and financially, business has tended to become a series of closed corporations with growing political influence over the legislature. As capitalist antagonisms have sharpened throughout the world, bankers have joined industrialists in demanding political support for the profit on price system in the home market; the trust has given birth to the tariff. So Tammany came to London town. It remains enthroned despite the economic tribulation and the threat to the peace of nations implied by its very presence.

The recommendation of the Committee on Trusts that the Board of Trade should be kept fully informed of the influence of trusts, should have power to compel information and, when a prima-facie case had been made, should publish such information and suggest appropriate State action, is a dead letter. The proposal of the Royal Commission on Food Prices that somebody "should be equipped with power to deal with monopolies, trusts, and combines which charge unduly high prices" has been mocked. Only one clear challenge is offered to monopoly. It is made by the Coöperative Movement's practicing its own principle of price without profit and safeguarding all consumers from the excessive toll of the trust.

VIII.

The Wilderness of Distribution

SHOPKEEPING is the last refuge of individual enterprise in an industrial civilization. Men turn to it inspired by enterprise, by the desire for independence, by the thrill of a speculation in which, they hope, personal labor will lend an element of security to personally owned capital; and because of concentration capital has destroyed adventure for the small man and rendered wage-paid employment insecure, the number of retail outlets grows and grows, making of distribution a maze that is still uncharted.

Price maintenance was the first and obvious demand of capitalists intent upon perfecting the technique of production. They formed their price rings and cartels. They reached backward to the sources of raw material. But they did not reach forward to distribution. So long as the expansion of industry induced the nation to be fruitful and to multiply, so long as the market continued buoyant, efficiency in retailing remained the last care of business.

The trend toward rationalization, historically, proceeded through the factory to merchandizing and wholesaling. Even now it has not really touched retailing, where tentative beginnings are being made only under pressure of the need for sustaining profit upon price. The Linlithgow Committee, while condemning the tendency toward trustification in the production and distribution of essential foodstuffs, complained about the myriad of middlemen and retailers standing between producer and consumer, and concluded that "taken as a whole, distributive costs are a far heavier burden than Society permanently will consent to bear." The simple truth is that there was no urge to match the monopoly of production with rationalization of distribution in a system

lacking a social ideal. Price fixing gave manufacturers all they
wanted. In distribution competition might continue to sur-
vive on condition that it was not unfettered.

Forty years ago an aspiring Free Trade M.P. observed
that the profits of proprietary articles, then enjoying a rising
demand through consumer stimulation by newspaper advertising, were being restricted in the cut and thrust of a free
retail market. He launched a Proprietary Articles Trade Association with these objects:

(a) The discussion of matters of common interest to the
branches of the trades represented, with a view to decision,
and, if necessary, concerted action.

(b) The taking of such steps as the Association may be
advised are legal to deal with extreme cutting of prices, and
to give advice and render assistance to its members in preventing substitution.

(c) The doing of such other things as may appear to be
of benefit to the trade.

Benefit to the trade is secured by insisting that the rate of
profit to wholesalers and retailers is adequate, the retail rate
for medicinal articles purchased in ordinary quantities from
wholesalers being 25 per cent. Before obtaining supplies the
wholesaler and retailer must sign an agreement not to sell
the goods below the fixed price. Breach of this agreement
brings a "stop list" into operation. Every manufacturer and
wholesaler in membership undertakes to withhold supplies
from firms on the "stop list."

In this way internal tariff walls have been erected round
4,000 articles in everyday use, from floor polish to baby
foods, and the price of commodities like aspirin has been inflated by several hundred per cent for the enrichment of the
manufacturer, the wholesaler, the retailer and the Press.
Here is the voice of Sir W. Glynn Jones, its founder and
secretary, expounding in February, 1923, the policy of the
P.A.T.A.: "In order to protect an article there must be someone who is able to control the supplies and turn the tap off.

You must, therefore, have someone in the end who is in a position of saying, 'You shall not have any more of my goods . . .' The principle is then, 'Cut one article and your supplies of the lot stop . . .' I am satisfied . . . that on these 4,000 articles at least £1,000,000 has been saved to the trade."

Within ten years of its foundation, the P.A.T.A. felt strong enough to take the offensive against the consumer's Coöperative Movement. It decided that dividend on purchases, far from being the increment of mutuality, was a method of price cutting. It decreed that supplies would be withheld from retail coöperative societies unless either the dividend was added to the minimum fixed price of the commodity at the time of purchase, or no dividend at all was paid. The clear intentions of this policy, which has been pursued ever since, are to divert trade from coöperative to private stores and to render consumers powerless against the impositions of a vested interest. The reply of the Coöperative Movement has been to manufacture equivalent goods in its own factories; but the reign of the price cartel is still supreme in many parts of the realm of pills and face powder. A Grocery Proprietary Articles Trade Association works in the same way.

Not all cartels covering the British market are indigenous. Directed from Geneva, and owned largely by non-British capital, is the Phoebus S.A. Compagnie Industrielle pour le Développement de L'Éclairage, correlating the world interests of manufacturers of electric goods, pooling and protecting their patents and parceling out sales territories among its constituents in all parts of the globe. Its British constituents include the producers of branded electric lamp bulbs, organized in the Electric Lamp Manufacturers Association, of which a subcommittee of the Standing Committee on Trusts reported in 1920: "The Electric Lamp Manufacturers Association has been created primarily in the interests of three firms; the British Thomson-Houston Company, the General Electric Company and Messrs. Siemens Brothers. These impose onerous conditions upon other firms in the Association, e.g., a limitation of output upon licensees and a stipulation that the validity of their patents shall not be questioned or disputed.

"The limitation of output imposed upon licensees is contrary to the best interests of the industry and of the consumer . . ."

Such indignation as the licensees may feel is assuaged by the margins afforded them in the retail price of lamps. That price is now, and has been for a number of years, the highest in Europe. In 1932, for the most common type of lamp, it was 4s. 8d. in Great Britain against a "fair" price of 1s. in Sweden.[1] The larger the lamp the wider the difference between the monopoly price and the "fair" price. On a consumption of 53,000,000 lamps per annum the cartel's excess of receipts from British consumers is in the region of £2,000,-000.

Elma maintains its own private detective corps. Retailers who cut prices are refused supplies of other electric goods and appliances. State assistance to and regulation of electrical development, through an Electricity Commission, has expanded enormously the market for electric goods since 1926. But the State has left the consumer defenseless against the extortions of Elma. It has been the task of the Scottish C.W.S., in conjunction with the Swedish Coöperative Movement, to secure a section of the market in which monopoly conditions will not operate. A new £60,000 factory is being built at Shieldhall for the production of lamps which, it has been agreed, will not compete with the trust's products in the open market but to which the entire coöperative market will be available.

Strangely enough, price fixing has not changed the individualistic character of the retail trade. On the contrary as shopkeepers have become mere factors of the packeted, fixed-

1. The dramatic story of the Swedish Coöperative Movement's battle with the Lamp Trust is told in *Sweden: The Middle Way*, by Marquis W. Childs.

price commodities, as "minding the dump" has become the essential function of shopkeeping, the business has attracted more unskilled men, and the chaos of distribution has become worse confounded. It is true that war is waged on the small shop by many and powerful competitors. It is true that in the years 1930–32, 10,000 small shopkeepers went bankrupt for sums aggregating £15,000,000. Between 1920 and 1930, however, the number of retail outlets rose from 600,000 to 750,000, and in the ten years till 1931 the number of new residential shops assessed for the first time for income tax doubled, while similar data for lock-up shops showed an increase of only 25 per cent. Price fixing for private profit has aggravated many of the strains and stresses of the economic system. Manufacturers have been enabled to "invent" fresh tastes in the confident hope that admission to old cartels or the creation of new ones will guarantee their prices and that lavish advertising will sell any kind of article, good, bad or indifferent, to the public. After comparing the price lists of a representative wholesale grocer for 1925 and 1935, Lord Luke of Pavenham reported to the Congress of the International Chambers of Commerce (1935) that he found thirty branded furniture and floor polishes as against fifteen, thirty-two proprietary cereal foods as against seventeen and, in twenty of the most important types of commodities, an increase of 43 per cent in the number of proprietary "lines which the grocer might reasonably be expected to carry."

Department stores, carrying great stocks of fixed-price goods, have flourished by use of a subtle technique of "service," drawing the patron to listen to lectures, see a cabaret, meet her friends, obtain ideas for the home and return handsome profits to the proprietors on incidental purchases. "The modern department store is carrying twice as many different kinds of things as it did fifteen years ago," Mr. Gordon Selfridge told the 1934 annual meeting of Selfridge Provincial Stores, Ltd., adding: "One hosiery department in our organisation has 10,764 different kinds of stockings. We have 12,-

000 different kinds of gloves, 5,000 different kinds of hand-
kerchiefs, 4,000 different kinds of handbags, and 135 different kinds of toothbrush." These department stores,
whether situated in the West End of London or the main
streets of provincial towns, aim at the luxury market. Their
counterparts in enterprise of the Woolworth, Marks and
Spencer type have invaded "poverty market" with "nothing
over 6d." goods. Whether or no the rapid spread of such
businesses has been forced by insurance companies and other
investors of finance capital, the effects of price fixing are
clear: costly new distributive agencies, inflating land and
capital values, have been superimposed upon the crazy, out-
dated structures of the retail trade.

Rationalization of wholesaling has contributed very little
to a reduction of the hypertrophy of selling. In the drapery
trade, especially, its main effect has been to add to the number of magnificent buildings, expensively equipped, decorat-
ing the country's shopping centers. When the Drapery Trust
ringed Great Britain from Piccadilly, London, to Sauchie-
hall Street, Glasgow, its aim was to centralize the buying for
twenty-six companies, the majority of which had acquired
monopoly status in local centers. Immediately, wholesalers
in the drapery trade combined to safeguard their own position. They insisted upon manufacturers selling through them
to the small trader on the same terms that the trust could
command. An integral relationship between big retailers and
wholesalers was encouraged on one hand. Side by side there
grew up an integral relationship between manufacturers and
a section of the wholesalers serving small retailers. The status
quo was preserved, except for the consumer. He was placed
at the mercy of stronger competing groups than formerly.

Another interesting aspect of the retail problem is the
ownership of branch stores by manufacturers whose products
are already protected by P.A.T.A. and similar price agreements. Multiple drug stores, financed by drug makers, for
example, are as common on street corners as branch banks;

and the four largest of these groups operate £11,250,000 of aggregate capital, 1,800 branches and 30,000 employees. These companies are enthusiastic about consumer research. They conduct experimental shops in which attempts are made to test demand scientifically and to study consumer reactions at first hand. Yet beyond concentrating the sale of their own products in their own shops and eliminating some of the overhead charges involved in commissions to travelers, they have failed to influence profoundly the progress of distribution in a planned, orderly way. What they, and the direct-to-consumer makers of footwear and clothing and woolen goods and sewing machines have done is to increase the aggressiveness of their own sales force, to add more and louder voices to the many raucous noises assailing the ears of the purchasing public.

The one definite effort to rationalize distribution has been made by manufacturers of those high-priced products of which the popularity depends to some extent upon the technical service offered to purchasers. These firms, instead of producing for all retailers willing to handle their goods, have themselves applied the principle of selectivity to distributive outlets. By concentrating sales in fewer and fewer hands, they have achieved certain of the economies of an organized market for themselves and the retailers whom they favor, and have encouraged a high mortality rate among those small shopkeepers against whom they boycott. In no instance have any of the principal manufacturers of goods in this field—radios, phonographs and cameras—chosen coöperative societies as their distributors. Faced with the difficulty that, whether in town or village, coöperative societies tend more and more to dominate the market, they have applied P.A.T.A. regulations to sales and refused supplies unless societies accept the condition that a dividend must not be paid on these products. The reply of the Coöperative Movement has been to manufacture its own phonographs, to market a high quality radio set the parts of which are produced by noncombine firms and assembled in coöperative workshops, to encourage independent suppliers of cameras and photographic films to cater to the coöperative trade and, so far as tariffs will permit, to draw upon imports. Patent and copyright laws have hampered coöperative efforts to defeat these forms of boycott, since the making of phonograph records, for example, is an essential ancillary to the production of phonographs and the best artists are bought up by the big companies; but the coöperative check upon what otherwise would be an all-inclusive monopoly becomes increasingly effective.

Vigorously anticoöperative in policy are the 5,500 shops grouped in the Home and Colonial Stores, Ltd., and dominated by the world-wide Unilever Combine. Amalgamation, absorption and agreement have brought the Maypole Dairy Company, Ltd., the Meadow Dairy Company, Ltd. (which includes Brough's, Ltd., Sherry's Dairy Company, Neale's Tea Stores, Ltd., and Pearks Dairies, Ltd.), and Lipton's, Ltd., into close association. Their warehousing and wholesaling is concentrated in Allied Suppliers, Ltd., owning a London tea-packing plant with a capacity exceeding 1,000,-000 lbs. per week. They are said to be "on excellent terms" with the family firm of J. Sainsbury, Ltd., which, in turn, has an agreement to avoid competition with David Greig, Ltd. In 1930 an unsuccessful bid was made to link the Home and Colonial with the remaining outstanding national multiple[2] in the grocery trade, International Tea Stores, which, with the Star Tea Company, Ltd., provides 1,000 retail outlets for the potted meat, pickles and jams of Kearley and Tonge, Ltd.

Between the growing number of multiples and the Coöperative Movement battle is fierce and unending. Double-weight margarine, free soap with ham or free packets of cheese with sugar are the alternatives to dividends on purchases offered by the multiples both national and local. Occasionally they obtain great consignments of cheap bread or

2. i.e., chain store.

greengroceries, which they do not sell ordinarily, and cut retail prices in the hope of attracting trade in cheese and butter, ham and eggs from the coöperative store. The effect upon small retailers has been devastating enough. Even the governmental inquiry which recommended the taxation of coöperative funds admitted that "the elimination of the small trader is due as much (if not more) to the increasing number of multiple shops and departmental stores as to the growth of co-operative societies." The Coöperative Movement itself, however, has remained almost unimpaired. To meet attack, its price policy has become more flexible. A coöperative manager or committee, generally, will not seek to provoke attack. When attack is precipitated, a frequent reaction is to reduce prices over a range of commodities in accord with the policy of retaining public confidence by giving consumers their dividend at the time of purchase instead of as a deferred rebate; and the frequency of assault has directed the attention of co-operators to the need for amalgamation and joint action among themselves. Moreover, the expansion policy pursued by the multiples has not taken the form of buying up existing businesses and modernizing existing shops but of opening new premises and adding to the already excessive number of existing outlets. Thus the ratio of fixed investments to total investments has risen and with it there has risen the ratio of expenses. A marked tendency of recent years has been for the multiples to concentrate upon the faster selling fixed-priced commodities to the detriment of the department stores and to stimulate a form of competition which, while it does not affect the money in the housewives' purse, does influence in what type of shop her money will be spent. Whether its own leaders consider the multiple-store method efficient and economic is not quite certain. Ten weeks after his election as chairman of the Home and Colonial, able financial adviser and diplomat Sir George E. Schuster, K.C.S.I., K.C.M.S., C.B.E., M.C., told the annual meeting[3] that a policy of de-

3. March 25, 1936.

centralization had been adopted to meet the problems of a decline in turnover "not merely in values owing to the fall in the general price level, but also in quantities" during the years 1930–34, and proceeded to "think aloud" on the "general idea that our shops are now on wrong lines and cannot compete with the larger stores which show a much greater diversity of articles." Sir George admitted the powerful competition of such stores, and concluded: "In the first place you should appreciate that we have in our group several examples of companies still running the smaller specialty shop in a successful and profitable manner . . . In the second place, we cannot suddenly change our character. Our shops are adapted to a certain kind of business and, if we try suddenly to force them to do a business for which they are not adapted, we may well fall between two stools and get into real confusion." Incidentally, the Home and Colonial chairman observed that "the effects of the decline in turnover were for the years 1931–34 to some extent mitigated by an increase in the margin of gross profit retained on sales." He did not reveal whether this profit margin was increased through the fall in wholesale prices or the maintenance of fixed retail prices or both.

Despite the move toward amalgamation among coöperative societies and the tendency toward standardization of prices—which contrasts sharply with capitalist price fixing, since coöperative societies do not fix prices in order to obtain profits but to achieve economies which are returned to consumers—the local character of coöperative storekeeping continues to distinguish it from its multiple shop rivals. Every autonomous coöperative society tends to be related closely to the size and character of the district it serves. Springing spontaneously from the needs of the people, it grows in tune with changing public demand, naturally and economically.

A village society with a few hundred members will conduct all its trade from a single village store, perhaps departmentalizing that one store in response to modern requirements, but branching out only slowly and only to meet a known and assured market. There the local draper and the local ironmonger are probably good coöperators buying, like everybody else in the village, their foodstuffs from the "coöp" which, in turn, is reluctant to invade the draper's or the ironmonger's territory. At the other extreme is a giant society like London, facing fearlessly the competition of thousands of independent shops, chain stores, department stores and maximum price fancy goods stores, and itself conducting a large chain store service radiating from a number of big emporiums.

In 1935 there were 399 retail coöperative societies with less than 1,000 members each, 565 societies ranging between 1,001 and 10,000 members, 132 societies with memberships between 10,001 and 50,000, and 22 societies with more than 50,000 members. Between the pigmies and the giants are a countless variety of types, from regional societies with one suite of shops in a market town and a series of traveling vans traversing hundreds of square miles, to societies possessing the most imposing central stores in many large cities and serving provincial suburbia through a series of small branch department stores.

The range of goods and services offered, although uniform in quality, is as numerous as the types of societies. Some societies do not sell furniture and clothing. Others do not sell milk or meat or bread or coal. The foundations of important new coöperative retail federal societies have been laid in the arrangements made by some small societies to enable their members to buy fashion goods at the nearest large society. Of these large societies it may be said that there is nothing they do not sell. They provide baby with its milk, its cot, its carriage, its toys and its penny savings bank. They provide mother with every kind of "convenience goods" from bread and meat to tinned fruits and sweets and father's tobacco. They offer a variety of "shopping goods" like dress and furniture—with café service and music and manikin parades—

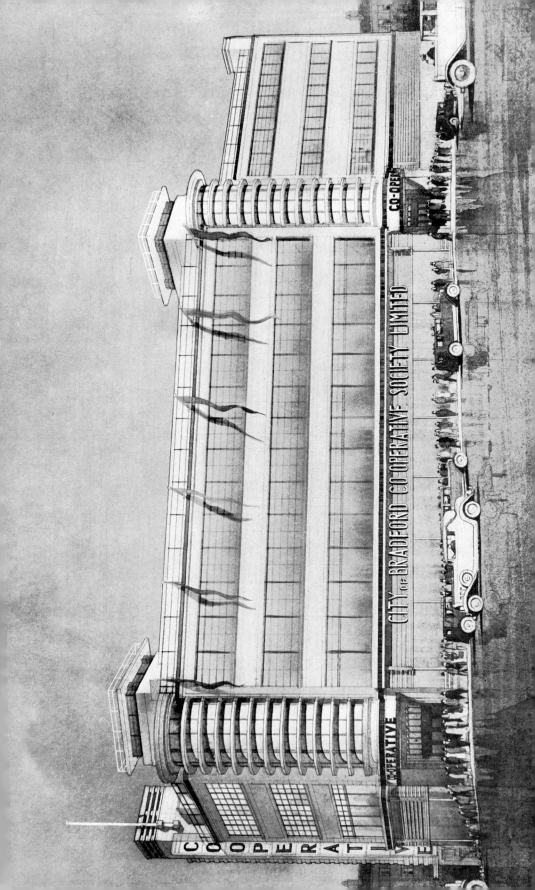

Central premises of the City of Bradford Co-operative Society, Ltd., designed by the C.W.S. Architects Department equal to any of their rivals. They have on display almost everything the consumer wants in the way of "speciality goods" like vacuum cleaners and bicycles; a coöperative society gave the first retail store display of television in Great Britain. Associated with them are optical departments, travel bureaus, house-building departments and agencies of the C.W.S. National Health Approved Society, through which individual coöperators may pay their contributions to National Health Insurance and widows' and orphans' pension funds.

This local character of retail Coöperation is not conducive to forced expansion or rapid change. Yet it helps to preserve the democracy of the coöperative system. It renders a trade organization touching one in three British homes properly resistant to the unregulated output of branded foods and newfangled, largely unnecessary goods; and its development which, as the figures show, has been colossal, has been economic. It has not burdened the land with new shops, driving up its own and the community's overhead charges. Indeed, the fact that the stocks of distributive coöperative societies fell from the peak figure of £36,000,000 in the boom year of 1920, to £17,760,000 in 1934, while land, buildings and fixtures used in trade increased from £21,000,000 to £45,-000,000 and annual stock turnover rose from 6.9 per cent to 11.6 per cent is suggestive of much—that with more intensive departmentalization there has gone greater efficiency in stock control; that the clear lead coöperative stores established over all competitors in the "efficiency audits" conducted by governmental inquiries in the years 1919–24 has been maintained; that, in the fierce struggle yet to come with their multiple rivals, the capital policy of coöperative societies has yielded them an advantage which must give pause to all who would challenge their growing supremacy.

How many shops are there in Great Britain? What is the volume of retail trade, and the proportion passing through the several types of retail outlets? Nobody knows. There has been no census of distribution. Although the Briton, making a virtue of necessity, interprets the historical sneer that his is "a nation of shopkeepers" as a compliment, he is coy when asked to uncover the facts about the distributive trade; so coy that critics declare the facts do not bear examination.

We may, however, make a tentative attempt to chart the maze. There were certainly not less than 1,000,000 shops in 1935, one shop to every forty-five inhabitants compared with one shop to every seventy-nine inhabitants of the United States in 1929. These shops fall into three main categories. There are large shops, including the department stores, chain stores and bazaars. There are small shops comprising a tremendous variety of retail outlets from local chain store organizations to single residential shops. There are the coöperative societies. Of the large shops, the public corporations, which do not cover the whole field, may be grouped as follows: drapery and general stores with £46,000,000 of capital and 360 branches; grocery and provision shops with £24,000,000 of capital and 9,000 branches; the meat combine (the Vestey Trust, of which the controlling body is the Union Cold Storage Company, Ltd., owners of a line of steamships, cattle ranches, warehouses and a complete transport system) and a few multiple butchers with £14,000,000 capital and 5,500 branches; drug stores with £11,250,000 capital and 1,800 branches; dairies with £6,000,000 capital and 800 branches; boot and shoe companies with £12,-500,000 and 2,500 branches; gentlemen's tailors with £12,-000,000 and 1,400 branches; furniture firms with £3,250,-000 capital and 100 branches; tobacconists (some of them controlled by the big productive combines) with £1,500,000 capital and 1,100 branches; bazaars with £12,000,000 and 750 branches; and miscellaneous companies selling commodities like wool and sewing machines with £7,500,000 and 5,-000 branches.[4]

Let us glance at the numerous estimates of experts, assum-

4. Hoffman, *Shops and the State*, p. 9 *et seq.*

ing that the volume of retail sales in 1934 was £2,056,000,-
000 and remembering always that there are no absolutely
reliable figures covering the entire distributive trade. Subject
to that qualification, it would appear that 750,000 small
shops did 66 per cent (£1,358,000,000) of the trade; that
department stores and multiple firms, with 40,000 shops did
19 per cent (£411,000,000) of the trade, the figures for the
multiples, as distinct from the department stores, being 12.5
per cent (£257,000,000) of the trade in 39,000 shops; and
that the Coöperative Movement did just over 10 per cent
(£207,000,000) of the trade in 15,000 shops. A "break-
down" of these figures covering 95 per cent of retail trade
is interesting. It indicates that 30 per cent of the retail trade
is done in 6 per cent of the shops for which we have accounted,
and that the turnover per retail outlet per annum is as follows: coöperative society, £13,800; multiple, £6,590; small
shop, £1,810. This "break-down" also points to differential
standards in turnover and profit and service, deep and widespread enough to constitute a grave indictment against the
organization of distribution in modern Britain.

Beyond all doubt there is a misuse of labor in the distributive trade so reckless that the more reputable employers are
now associating themselves with the agitation, sustained by
the Coöperative Movement for forty years, to remove the
stigma of sweating from a major industry. Between 1923
and 1934, the number of distributive workers insured by the
State against unemployment increased from 1,260,000 to
2,000,000. In one decade, of the total number of insured
workers, the proportion represented by the distributive trades
swelled from 11 per cent to 15.5 per cent. Omitting transport
workers, clerks and restaurant employees, of every seven
British workers one is engaged in selling the goods produced
by the other six.

Comparisons drawn from England and Wales Occupation
Tables in the 1921 and 1931 Censuses show that the army
of commercial travelers rose from 83,000 to 122,000, can-

vassers (not including dock, insurance or railway) from 5,-800 to 34,000, salesmen and shop assistants from 660,000 to 965,000, and employers and managers of wholesale and retail businesses from 540,000 to 651,000. Neither juveniles under sixteen years of age, nor employees in receipt of over £250 per annum, nor working proprietors, came within the scope of the official figure of 2,000,000 insured employees. Estimating juveniles at 100,000,[5] those in receipt of more than £250 a year at 50,000 and, on the assumption that, as in America, "proprietors and firm members" amount to one third of the total number of employees, working proprietors at 700,000, there are between 2,750,000 and 3,000,000 persons engaged directly in wholesale and retail distribution. Of every twenty-four persons in the United States, one hands out goods to the other twenty-three. Of every seventeen persons in Great Britain, one hands out goods to the other sixteen.

Price fixing has tended to equalize competition between the same type of commodities. Thus the incidence of competition in the distributive trade falls elsewhere. It falls partly on the shop premises. These must bear heavy overhead charges—difficult to pass on to consumers—in respect of fittings and services designed to attract customers; fittings and services which add to site value and raise valuation upon which local rates are paid. More particularly, the incidence of competition falls upon the overworked and underpaid shop assistant. Outside the Coöperative Movement and a few better-class chain stores, trade union organization among shop assistants is almost unknown. The rate of labor turnover may be gauged from the fact that, in a continuously expanding industry, unemployment was 223,000 in April, 1934, compared with 76,000 in January, 1922. The absorption by cooperative retail societies of 32,000 additional distributive

5. Juveniles are now insured. The Ministry of Labor report for 1935 classes 246,000 persons under sixteen as being engaged in distribution—25 per cent of the total number of insured juvenile workers!

workers into secure employment over that period throws the
facts into even more lurid relief. There is little doubt that
shop assistants themselves are appreciative of the significance
of the Coöperative Movement's efforts to mitigate their
plight. Private trade organizations complain that the bulk of
wages earned in private shops is spent in coöperative stores.
They apply pressure to prevent shop assistants from shopping coöperatively.

In 1930, when juniors in London were working 69 to 73
hours per week, and adult assistants were in receipt of 24s.
for a 74-hour week, the rates paid by the London Coöperative Society and members of the London Employers' Association for a 48-hour week ranged from 13s. at 14 years of age
to 66s. at 25, the coöperative employees having an advantage
of 7s. a week at 21, 5s. at 22, and 1s. at 23 over their fellows
in the best private trade houses. These differences were repeated throughout the country. How great is the gulf between coöperative and the more reputable private stores on
the one hand, and the majority of distributive stores on the
other, is indicated by the complaint of the National Amalgamated Union of Shop Assistants, Warehousemen and Clerks
that, in 1935, adult male shop assistants in thousands were in
receipt of less than 25s. per week, adult women were getting
25s. to 20s., while 35s. was a maximum figure for branch shop
managers. Investigating the conditions of grocery assistants
in 654 towns in 1924, the Ministry of Labor found that
whereas 84.6 per cent of coöperative employees were organized in trade unions, only 2.4 per cent of private trade employees were so organized. The effect of lack of trade union
organization was revealed in 1925 in a Ministry of Labor
report that 43 per cent of girls aged 16 received less than
15s.; 25 per cent aged 21 received less than 25s.; and nearly
50 per cent aged 23 received less than 30s. Since this information was supplied voluntarily, it is a safe assumption that
the worst employers withheld data and that the figures, de-
plorable as they are, were weighted by the returns of co-

operative societies and the few private firms then recognizing trade union standards.

A series of Government commissions, although abortive in their results, have shown that if the shop assistant's pocket is light, his head is made heavy enough by long hours. In 1892 legislation enforced a week of 74 hours inclusive of meal time for employees under 18 years of age. Forty-four years were to elapse before, in December, 1936, legislation fixed the hours of children at 48 per week, abolished overtime for those between the ages of 14 and 16, and limited overtime for those between the ages of 16 and 18. This legislation followed the report of a Select Committee on Shop Hours (1931) which declared that "in a great number of trades, the majority of assistants worked between 48 and 60 hours a week"; that excessive hours—"excessive" meaning over 60 per week—were possible and that "out of a large number of shop assistants chosen at random on Mersey side, 15 per cent worked over 60 hours per week." While closing orders have proved to be a partial boon providing benefits like the weekly half holiday in 1912 (of which the Coöperative Movement was a powerful advocate), these are fixed locally and usually by the small trader exercising a majority vote on local authorities. In some towns "closing time" is 7 P.M. In others it is 8 P.M. on four days, 9 P.M. on another with a weekly half holiday on a sixth day. In most towns, confectioners and tobacconists may remain open till 9.30 P.M. and 10 P.M. on Saturday. What poor protection such local legislation has given shop assistants has been destroyed by lack of national overriding legislation to prevent staffs from being worked after the shops are closed to the public.

Price fixing, of course, does not mean that excessive prices constitute the only burden of economic chaos borne by consumers. Every legitimate cost that can be passed on is passed on besides many that are not legitimate at all. Although the official testing of weights and measures, coupled with the stern opposition of the Coöperative Movement to such malpractices as including the weight of the package with the weight of the commodity, has gone some way toward safeguarding all consumers, a Food Council Report on Short Weight and Measure in 1926 deplored the extent to which Great Britain "lags behind in the elementary business of securing that the consumer gets what he asks for and pays for." "Nor does it accord with commonsense," the report went on, "that, while elaborate machinery is established by law to ensure that sellers should provide themselves with correct scales, weights and measures, no provision should exist for ensuring that the quantity of foodstuffs actually sold should be what they are represented to be, with the two exceptions of bread and tea," both of which owe their special position almost entirely to coöperative agitation and example. One of the cases upon which the Food Council based its report was that of a large firm retailing milk in bottles reputed to hold a pint. More than half of the bottles tested could not possibly hold that quantity, and the Council concluded that the firm was making £1,400 a year from the sale of milk it did not supply! No less than twenty-two recommendations were then made to strengthen the law against dishonest trading. These recommendations have not yet been embodied in law.

Adulteration and misdescription of commodities are rife, providing not only evidence that improper practices are prevalent and that the law is inadequate, but that lack of consumer education and the close financial relationship between the Press and commerce has rendered the British people singularly gullible. Public analysts, under the Ministry of Health, operate the negative function of testing samples of food and reporting upon their quality. When, as sometimes happens, legal action is taken and a conviction is secured, newspapers are inclined to treat such news as "bad news" and to ignore it, especially if it reflects upon the products of national advertisers. Yet the annual statements of the Ministry of Health contain numerous examples of sample tests revealing frauds as menacing to honest traders as to public health.

In 1935, the reports on eight samples of tea were unfavorable. Iron filings were present. Tea described as being free from injurious tannin contained 13.9 per cent. Seven samples of "cream" cheese were whole milk cheeses. In two samples sold as "double cream" cheese the principal ingredient was water.

The proprietary medicine business flourishes as profitably in Great Britain as in America. Lysol of British Pharmacopoeia standard—that is, the standard determined by a committee of doctors appointed by the General Medical Council and the Board of Trade—should contain 50 per cent by volume of cresol. Tests made on nine samples showed less than 3 per cent of cresol and, though labeled as being adequate solutions, when used in the proportions in which lysol is used ordinarily, these samples would have had no germicidal action. Patent medicines pretending to be "secret remedies" and issued to the public without a printed formula must be stamped under the Drug Acts. Governmental interest is concerned less with the formula than with attempts at evasion of payment of stamp duty. It is quite a common experience of the observant consumer to find on the shelves of the same drug store, say, three bottles of medicine produced by the same firm and claiming in newspaper advertisements similar curative properties, of which one will be stamped and carry no printed formula, two will be unstamped and labeled with formulæ, but the two formulæ will be different. With a tax of 3d. in every shilling, the stamp duty should yield roughly £3,500,000 on patent medicine sales aggregating £15,000,-000 per annum. The actual yield is about £750,000.

Food standards enforced by law are few. They include bread, the ingredients of which were fixed a century ago, butter to which coloring matter may be added, cream which has no minimum fat content, milk, condensed and dried milk, cheese, margarine, and, for fiscal purposes, tea, coffee, whisky, brandy, rum and gin.

The drive toward Protection has been accompanied by an

effort to induce farmers to apply grading methods and improve the quality of British agricultural products through a voluntary National Mark scheme. The scheme applies to some sections of the beef industry in which, owing to the operation of the 1934 Cattle Subsidy, grading has assumed a new importance, subsidy payments being based upon quality. The National Mark may be applied to eggs, poultry, fruit, vegetables, jam, butter, cheese and canned products. Blemishes must not appear, for example, on first-grade fruit. They may be allowed up to one half of a square inch on second-grade apples. Canned fruit, however, qualifies for the National Mark, not on the basis of the contents of the tin being fruit of National Mark standard but according to the variety of fruit used, the methods of preparation, and the observance of provisions as to packing. The one general recommendation is that prior to canning the fruit should be free from blemishes and defects. The value to consumers of the National Mark, which is administered by a quasi-judicial body appointed by the Minister of Agriculture, is negligible. It has been, in effect, more of an experiment in "Buy British" salesmanship than an attempt to safeguard consumers against exploitation.

In 1934, a Departmental Committee on the Composition and Description of Food complimented certain manufacturers, including the Coöperative Movement, on the quality of their food products and held that "the case for the extension of standards or definitions to all articles of food is not made out." This Committee, however, also suggested that "the law relating to the composition and description of articles of food should be altered so as to enable definitions to be described, or declarations of composition to be required, for articles of food other than liquid milk," and it drew attention to the importance of requiring a declaration of content for all foods especially offered for invalids and infants. The Minister of Health has ignored the suggestion of the Committee appointed by himself.

In America the volume of instalment selling preceding the slump of 1929 was boosted by businessmen as contributing to a new era of prosperity and planned distribution. The view of the British Department of Overseas Trade was different. It regarded "this 6,000 million dollars of instalment sale, or at least three-fourths of it," as representing "debt inflation." How far instalment selling has caused debt inflation in Great Britain is beyond computation. But its extent indicates that this system of inducing the consumer to mortgage his future earnings in order to satisfy present needs was forced by the failure of the poverty market to absorb goods carrying prices fixed at high levels, especially luxury goods like radios, vacuum cleaners and motor cars, and that the entire system has produced a new series of social and economic maladjustments. It has added heavily to the hypertrophy of selling. Referring to "the great redundancy of effort" in the selling of any product nowadays, motor magnate Lord Austin in January, 1935, pointed out that the motor industry spent hundreds of thousands of pounds each year in advertising, a cost which, together with other selling expenses, had to be included in the price of the car, but did not add one iota to the intrinsic value or quality of the product. Specific information is difficult to obtain, but it is on record that in the last ten years, while manufacturing costs have fallen considerably, the direct selling costs of a well-known firm of vacuum cleaner manufacturers have risen from 50 per cent to 60 per cent, and it is claimed that trade discounts (wholesalers and retailers' margins only) on wireless receiving sets rarely amount to less than 50 per cent of the price paid by the consumer. It is a self-evident proposition that the cost of interest on money locked up in goods sold by hire-purchase, plus the cost of credit inquiry, collections, bad debts, obtaining repossession when customers fail to maintain payment, reconditioning and resale must be added to the price charged for all products, whether sold on instalment or not: and the existence of price-fixing agreements makes easy the levering up of prices against all consumers to levels guaranteeing a "spread" sufficient to cover every new contingency introduced by manufacturers and wholesalers into retail selling. Moreover, the sale of speciality goods under agreements which the mass of the consuming public is unable to comprehend cannot be regarded as less evil than the sale of fish paste and patent medicine under false or misleading labels. In the rush for business, salesmen may be tempted to describe a farm laborer in Cumberland earning 30s. a week as a dairy manager. When the inevitable happens and the purchaser fails to keep up his payments, it is possible for the instalment firm, as for any other firm, to secure in a London court leave to issue process for recovery of a debt against the so-called dairy manager living three hundred miles away. The London court, from which knowledge of the real facts are withheld, may be satisfied that the purchaser can afford to travel south to contest the claim against him, may give judgment against him, may enrich the firm at the expense of the customer and by a gross abuse of its own process. There is also a clear duty devolving upon time-payment firms to insure that the purchaser appreciates the terms of the contract he has signed and to avoid any danger that their advertisements might mislead potential customers. Many judicial statements justify the view that the practice of misrepresenting the status of the purchaser is not infrequent, and that the duty just outlined is not always discharged.

Coöperative societies entered the business of hire-purchase tardily. They had an instinctive dislike of credit trading and of methods of salesmanship which, though profitable from the viewpoint of the seller, were uneconomic to the consumer and open to obvious abuse. There was, too, a feeling that new and doubtful forms of trade should not be permitted to interfere with the natural development of Coöperation. After years of heart searching, and under the compelling conviction that neglect of the time-payment system was deflecting trade to their competitors and enabling a potential social evil to grow unchecked, many societies tackled the furniture, drapery and other trusts which had turned tallyman. Experiments in shilling clubs were conducted by the Women's Coöperative Guild. They proved that coöperative "mutuality clubs" could avoid the dangers to which private forms of hire-purchase are prone.

In the first place, most coöperators have a capital sum, whether large or small, in the books of coöperative societies, and to that extent are creditworthy. Secondly, the purpose of coöperative mutuality could be divorced from the problem of selling special commodities, it could be a service rather than a form of high-powered salesmanship, and no single article need be advanced in price to cover the additional costs involved in ordinary hire-purchase. Thirdly, bad debts of any kind, while they exist, are comparatively small in well-managed societies. Thus, trade promoted by mutuality does not require to be differentiated from the general trade of retail societies. The member is entitled to the same dividend on boots bought by mutuality as on butter bought for cash.

Today, hundreds of coöperative societies conduct mutuality clubs, the members of which pay their weekly contributions direct to the branch store or to collectors and buy what they will on the same terms as cash customers. The available statistics show a trend which can be regarded as general. In 1931, the total annual mutuality collection in Scotland was estimated at £611,000 of which less than £600 had to be written off as a bad debt and only £754 was doubtful. Throughout the Midlands of England no society had mutuality debts in excess of 1s. 8d. per £100. In a total mutuality turnover of £771,000, a big English retail society had a total loss of only £100. Many variants of mutuality, even to hire-purchase itself, may be found now in the Coöperative Movement. Hire-purchase is applied only to high-priced articles and usually upon such terms that the interest charge borne by the consumer is canceled by treating his repayments as purchase qualifying for dividend.

The strength and simplicity of the Coöperative Movement reveal, by contrast, the curse of the price-fixing system—the curse of concealment. In the moderate industrial recovery stimulated by Protection, subsidies and large-scale rearmament, which reached its peak in December, 1936, distributive industrial shares, according to the Actuaries Investment Indices (December 31, 1928 equals 100), showed a rise in twelve months of 16.1 per cent compared with 11.8 per cent for industrial shares and 12 per cent for all classes of ordinary shares. Under these circumstances, the reformer who points to the fact that, as productive industry atrophies, there is an acceleration of the overgrowth of selling, is scorned. Nor is there a better fate for those few economists who see that, since profit is the magnet which attracts production in the capitalist system, profit is an essential regulating factor in that system and, when prices and profits are sustained at artificial levels by lopsided legislation, the one factor safeguarding the system from certain collapse loses its potency. It is not surprising that much salesmanship in Great Britain is waste. The position was well stated in a paper read in 1931 before the Centenary Meeting of the British Association by an advertising executive.[6] He cited the case of a manufacturer of a food product with a general distribution among shops in three different trades. On analysis, this manufacturer found that 56 per cent of his total sales force expense was incurred in selling to one of those trades which brought him only 12 per cent of his sales volume. Some of his salesmen were calling on shops where the sales cost was greater than the value of the sales made. On the whole, it was costing him in sales-force expense alone over 60 per cent of the return he got from that trade. Another manufacturer found that 6 per cent

6. Edward B. Gordon of The J. Walker Thompson Company.

of the 1,700 shops at which his travelers were calling did 50 per cent of the total sales volume.

Apart from the problems raised by the vulgarity of the technique used by many advertisers, "manufacturers," the British Association was told, "are wasting vast sums of money in advertising each year because they have no accurate knowledge of consumer markets or of the media for reaching these markets." In one investigated sample over 85 per cent of the expense—representing 2 per cent of the retail price—of sending out display material to retailers was waste; the retailers did not use the material. In the search for greater volume, too, many manufacturers added new lines of merchandise which ultimately resulted in a loss of prior economies secured by standardization and mass production. Of twenty-five lines produced by a manufacturer, eight represented over 95 per cent of his volume. Because of the economy of salesmen's time, more concentrated advertising, reductions in factory costs, shipping-room expense and so on, this manufacturer could have made a greater profit by dropping seventeen lines completely. The key words are "a greater profit."

Behind the retail shop stand the wholesale markets. These have changed but little since governmental committees condemned Covent Garden, London's fruit and vegetable depot, as "a confused and unorganised anachronism" and placed on record the story that it costs as much to distribute and retail a side of beef in the course of three days as it does to rear, feed and tend the animal for three years, transport its carcass, perhaps over thousands of miles of ocean, and pay a fair profit to those concerned, including the primary producer. Two years after the Linlithgow Committee administered its castigations, the "spread" between wholesale and retail prices of British Columbia box apples was 124 per cent, Nova Scotia barrel apples, 100 to 200 per cent, and Jaffa oranges 50 to 290 per cent. In milk, meat, bacon and potatoes, the same story repeats itself; middlemen are too thick on the ground. Yet agricultural Marketing Acts have been designed to increase and stabilize prices and to make profitable a discreditable chaos. In the result, while wages in insured trades in 1936 remained just below 1931 levels, when they were cut by £600,000 a week, the retail prices of essential foodstuffs had risen by not less than 25 per cent.

In 1931 the cost of distributing approximately £2,500,-000,000 worth of commodities from manufacturer to wholesaler then on to the retailer was £1,000,000,000, or approximately 40 per cent. All the evidence—of the growing number of small retailers whose custom is sought eagerly by a growing army of manufacturers' travelers, of the maintenance of price levels while mass purchasing power has declined, and of the increasing penetration of price-fixing cartels—points to a sharp rise in the cost of distribution since 1931. That is the price of muddle in the distributive trade. It is a problem to which only the British Coöperative Movement is as yet providing any answer.

IX.

The Law and the Profits

WHO shall rule, democracy or a dictator? That, a major issue of modern politics, is the essential issue of modern business and it is being decided today in favor of a dictator.

A coöperative society, like a joint-stock company, is an association of shareholders contributing a fund of capital to be employed under their collective direction. There the similarity ends, for the shareholders of a coöperative society are also its members, with a membership interest transcending their interest as shareholders. Their aim in trading is not to return interest, beyond a maximum rate fixed by rule, upon their shareholdings. It is to provide for their common needs as members and consumers, and to divide the saving arising from collective ownership and control as a patronage dividend. In a joint-stock company, the interest of the shareholder as a shareholder is, legally, paramount; the company's single aim in trading is to secure the highest return upon the shareholder's capital. These distinctions in purpose, as we shall see presently, reach down to the smallest detail of the operations of the two types of association. Yet examination reveals this paradox: that the difference between coöperative and joint-stock organization emerges most clearly in that matter in which their similarity should be most marked —the matter of collective direction of collective funds.

To deny some element of democracy to joint-stock finance would be unfair and, historically, inaccurate. Joint-stock finance sought to diffuse ownership in business ventures. It envisaged persons with surplus funds placing their money at the disposal of other capitalists and entrepreneurs on condition that the original owners retain a substantial measure

of control over the administration of their capital. Company
law entitles shareholders to attend and vote at meetings, to
elect directors and appoint auditors, to receive published accounts and, by special resolution, alter or add to the Articles
of Association of the business. Thus is preserved the legal
fiction that shareholders continue to exercise collective direction of their funds. The truth is that the success of the joint-
stock system has destroyed whatever elements of democracy
it ever boasted, and the legal assumptions no longer corre-
spond to the business realities.

How is it possible, to take an outstanding example, for Mr.
A, one of the 124,690 ordinary shareholders in Imperial
Chemical Industries, Ltd., to learn in person what is hap-
pening to the capital he has subscribed? Inquiry involves investigation of the affairs of the parent company, of more than
fifty other companies (themselves controlling fourteen more
subsidiaries) dominated by I.C.I., and of two companies (one
with another subsidiary) in which I.C.I. is interested with
other corporations. Although, as the Company Law Amendment Committee reported in 1926, the "great majority of
limited companies are honestly and conscientiously managed," under conditions of widely diffused capital ownership
control is almost certain to become concentrated in the hands
of "insiders" who may exercise effective power without necessarily acquiring a majority of shares. These "insiders" are
not charged with the task of developing a technique of democratic administration. Their task is to return profits upon
capital. In perfectly honest pursuit of that task, they have
sought to make their personal administrative positions im-
pregnable against the ignoramus and busybody to be found
in every group of shareholders, and have filched rights from
all shareholders, to the grave discredit of the joint-stock system. The result is the allocation of voting privileges to certain classes of shareholders, the formation of holding companies in which financial "genius" rather than shareholding

power predominates, and the creation of a financial dictator-ship. Since legislation does not endow shareholders with the means of exercising the powers which the law evidently in-tends that they should possess, the tendency toward dictator-ship in finance is unchallenged. For all practical purposes, indeed, the only right remaining to a shareholder in a pres-ent-day company is the right to hold a post-mortem on his lost savings.

Consider the case of the shareholder who desires to reform a private company. He is spurred to action as a result of losses already incurred. He is branded as an agitator animated by unworthy motives. The better founded his allegations, the more devastating on the Stock Exchange valuation of his own shares is the effect of the publicity he gives them. He in-volves himself in heavy costs in time and money. In a final circular sent out on June 24, 1929[1] by the Marconi Share-holders' Association which endeavored, unsuccessfully, to prevent Marconi capital's being written down from £7,213,-121 to £1,625,032, there was presented an audited bill of expenses amounting to £867 of which £763 was paid by the members of the Committee. The attempt to exercise post-mortem control besides being expensive, is seldom effective. Where, then, stands the auditor, appointed by the share-holders and responsible directly to them? His legal responsi-bility is to report to the proprietors or shareholders on the accounts examined by him. He must state whether he has obtained all the information and explanations he requires and whether, in his opinion, the balance sheet is properly drawn up so as to exhibit a true and correct view of the company's affairs according to the best of his information and the ex-planations given him, and as shown in the books of the com-pany. But the position here indicated, of the auditor acting as a guardian of the shareholders, has been modified by the decisions of the courts. His Majesty's judges have held that an auditor has nothing whatever to do with business policy,

1. Quoted in *Financial Democracy*, by Miller and Campbell, p. 35.

with prudence or efficiency; his duty is to ascertain and state the true financial position of the company at the time of the audit. "He is," in the words of a celebrated judgment, "a watchdog, but not a bloodhound."

A shock awaits the trusting investor who imagines that if his money gets into the hands of crooks and incompetents the law will intervene on his behalf, for the courts, which can be moved only when some part of his savings have vanished, are unlikely to afford him any real protection. Deliberate fraud, such as issuing a false prospectus, meets with swift punishment. A director may not falsify books, make secret profits, or be a party to a contract in which he has a personal interest without disclosing the nature of that interest to his fellow directors. Yet the court will hesitate to construe these obligations of agency and trusteeship in terms of negligence and inefficiency. Large powers of delegation to officials are accorded to directors. They will not be held liable for errors of judgment, nor will the degree of skill or diligence required of them be defined. The attitude of the court is that the company itself, by the terms of its Articles of Association and by the decisions of its general meeting, must assume all responsibility for electing efficient directors and supervising their activity. Indeed, in a case in which it was sought to make directors liable because, among other things, they had given an improvident loan to one of themselves, the judge held that "whatever may have been the amount lent to anyone, however ridiculous and absurd their conduct might seem, it was a misfortune of the company that they chose such unwise directors; but so long as they kept within the powers of the deed, the court could not interfere with the discretion exercised by them."[2]

How remote is the influence of the shareholder when a series of businesses is operated by a holding company was well illustrated by an effort at analysis of the position of the Unilever group made by the city editor of a London daily news-

2. *Turquand* v. *Maxwell* (1869), quoted in *Financial Democracy*, p. 68.

paper on April 13, 1934.[3] "Although the Unilever Combine may be, and very probably is, an exceedingly well managed concern," he wrote, "it is practically impossible for anyone to discover from the public accounts of the company, Unilever, Ltd., and Unilever N.V., and those of its associates and subsidiaries which are public concerns the true financial position of the whole group . . . no consolidated balance-sheet is published." Discussing the companies within the "world's most secretive combine," this city editor pointed out that the parent companies, which were public, were controlled by two small private companies: United Holdings, Ltd., and N.V. Elma. United Holdings, with £100,000 in one shilling deferred shares in Unilever, Ltd., out of a total issued capital of £14,138,750 possessed two million votes, whereas the £11,388,750 worth of ordinary shares carried only one vote for every £10 worth of shares, and the 2,720,-000 preferred shares carried votes only if their dividend was more than twelve months in arrears, and then only one vote for every ten shares. Thus the holders of £100,000 enjoyed a voting dictatorship. The Dutch Holding Company—N.V. Elma—owned 2,400 of one thousand florins each in Unilever N.V., out of a total issued capital of 204,284,500 florins. Every resolution passed by the general meeting of Unilever N.V. had to be ratified by the holders of these 2,400 shares. Dominating the two Unilever formations, these holding companies controlled also the subsidiaries of Unilever and, taking only the publicly owned securities of those companies which had shares or debentures issued on the London Stock Exchange, an aggregate of British capital in excess of £90,-000,000. "The owners of all this large amount of money," concluded the critic, "have not only no effective voice in the control of the group in which their savings are invested . . . but it is also practically impossible for them to obtain even the most scanty picture of the affairs of the group in which their money is invested."

3. *Daily Herald.*

One answer to this criticism is that, even if the technique of company control was brought into consonance with the historic spirit of joint-stock finance, the mass of shareholders are incapable of wise collective direction of their capital. In keeping with this view, many of the companies launched during the Stock Exchange boom of 1928, when an amended Company Act was in prospect, were floated on the basis of stockholders' putting up the bulk of the capital in nonvoting shares, while control was vested in ordinary shareholders providing only a small amount of capital in shares of low denominations. Regarded from any angle the answer, unlike too many shares now circulating, does not hold water: for it is a denial of every principle upon which Capitalism founds its case. It implies that a man, having built a business and turned it over to a public company, may exploit the joint-stock system in the interests of personal ownership. It transfers the element of money risk from those in command of business to the mass of shareholders which is, in fact, the whole community. It converts the rights of the shareholder into mere privileges and destroys his sense of duty. It makes of company finance a casino in which the great majority of honest businessmen are at a disadvantage, and crooks—who are numerous enough everywhere at any time—may make sport with the money of small investors.

Coöperation does not yet provide a complete answer to the challenge of the dictator in finance, but within the Movement itself democracy is in effective control of a mighty volume of capital.

An examination of the comparative positions of a group of shareholders registered under the Industrial and Provident Societies Acts, 1893 and 1913 (a coöperative society) and a group of shareholders registered under Company Law is instructive. The Society is registered with the Registrar of Friendly Societies, is registered with rules and, upon registration, pays a fee of £5 (which may be reduced in certain circumstances), irrespective of the amount of its capital. The company is registered with the Registrar of Joint-Stock Companies, is registered with a Memorandum of Association and Articles of Association, and pays for deed stamp and a registration fee, the amount of the fee depending upon the nominal share capital. A society comprises seven members, or two registered societies—this to enable federal societies to work—places no limit on the number of members it may accept and accords to every member one vote regardless of the number of shares he may hold. A private company requires two members and a public company seven members, the private company being limited in the number of members it admits. Both types of company permit votes according to the shares held by members. More numerous, and not less profound, are the distinctions in the treatment of capital by the two groups. The society limits the shareholding per member but, since membership is open, places no limit upon its total share capital. The company limits its total share capital, but places no limit upon the holding of the individual. Whereas the society may have either transferable or withdrawable shares, and can repay transferable shares, the company's shares are transferable only, and any repayment of share capital requires the sanction of the court. This is a distinction freeing coöperative shares from Stock Exchange speculation. The bulk of coöperative capital is withdrawable at the will of the member; much of it is withdrawable on call. Since the average coöperative member possesses as little knowledge of the technicalities of share transfer and of Stock Exchange jargon as the average member of a company, the advantage of the withdrawable share system is obvious; and the effect of share capital being invested or withdrawn at the will of the member, combined with open membership, is to prevent fluctuation in share values and to give coöperative investment a steadiness which neither the shares of companies nor of governments can achieve.

These safeguards of shareholders in coöperative societies are a barrier to the manipulation of shares, the formation of holding companies, the creation of any kind of financial dictatorship. The barrier is strengthened by the matters which, the Registrar insists, must be provided for in the society's rules, including the mode of holding meetings, the manner of making, altering or rescinding rules, and the appointment and removal of a committee of management, managers and other officers and their respective powers and remuneration. Among the statutory duties of the society is "making and keeping hung up the half-yearly statements required by the Act in the registered office and other places of business."

Now, it may be argued that these rules and regulations offer no solution to the problems which have caused the shareholder and control of his shareholding to become divorced in private business—the problems arising from the fact that shareholders are awakened to dangers only when inefficient administration of their affairs becomes palpable, that they are scattered and hard to organize, and that it is almost impossible to devise a technique which would induce at least an intelligent minority to participate actively in government and, in the phrase of an American economist, "cultivate ability by affording an opportunity for its exercise."

Inspection of the affairs of a coöperative society by the Registrar, who will take action on an application by one hundred members or one tenth of the membership if there are fewer than one thousand members, is rare. The members of a coöperative society are not scattered; they live within the boundaries of a society's trading area. They have presented to them half-yearly balance sheets which, in the main, are models of simplicity. In all societies they meet, not once a year, but twice a year. In most societies they meet quarterly and even monthly. No coöperative society throws up its hands at the physical impossibility of accommodating all its members if they desire to attend its meetings. It encourages them to attend by organizing district business meetings in its area and, where such sectional meetings are necessary, it is usual for directors to be elected on the basis of district representation. In short, a coöperative society has nothing to gain by secrecy and everything to lose by lack of publicity. Where members are apathetic, apathy is regarded as being a grave reflection on the society. Above all, coöperative business does what all reformers would have all business do in the modern world. It serves a social, communal aim. The many agencies which, as we have seen, spring spontaneously from the practice of Coöperation, are active promoters of democracy, jealous of its reputation. They bring to bear upon the affairs of their societies a constant surveillance which can, when occasion demands, provide a check upon inefficiency.

The rights and duties of the coöperative auditor who must be a Public Auditor approved by the Treasury, would not appear to be different from those of the auditor of a private company. The nature and organization of the coöperative membership, however, does give him a status and an independence envied by most auditors who, though nominally elected by the shareholders and responsible to them, are dependent upon the good will of directors and are bound to act with caution. Coöperative auditors usually play a large part in the affairs of the Coöperative Movement. In addition to meeting shareholders twice a year, they are also in regular consultation with committees of management and membership of a society is as open to an auditor as to anyone else. Coöperation, in short, does endeavor to relate the moral worth of the community to the organization of its business. In that relation lies one secret of security for capital and survival for the democratic spirit.

The powers enjoyed by a coöperative society registered under the Industrial and Provident Societies Acts are reasonably adequate. It can sue in its own name and hold property in its own name. It may enter into any business described in its rules except banking which, the law requires, must be conducted only on the basis of nonwithdrawable shares. It may engage in almost any type of business transaction, invest "any part of its capital in or upon any security authorized by its

rules," and it may make advances to its own members on the
security of real or personal property. It may also recover debts
from its members and exercise a lien upon a member's share
capital for debts owing to the society. The vital weaknesses
of the Acts, which coöperators have striven to remedy without success, are that individual holdings of capital are limited
to £200, that a society must fix in its rules a nominal limit
to the amount of loan capital it desires to raise, and that there
is no copyright in the name "Coöperation." "Coöperative"
societies of all descriptions muscle in upon the reputation for
probity built up by the Movement. There are "coöperative"
football pool societies engaging in betting on the results of
football matches. There are "coöperative" legal aid associations willing to take action on behalf of the victims of accidents on a promise to pay them 10 per cent of the damages
recovered, but withholding from prospective clients the fact
that failure in the courts will involve applicants in paying the
costs of the defendants. There are "coöperative" organizations for small investors enjoying the facilities of cheap registration and placing the small investor's money with companies that are among the Coöperative Movement's most
uncompromising enemies.

Following the recent appearance of Fixed Trusts claiming
to have attracted upward of £50,000,000 of small investors'
money for distribution among stated securities, there have
grown property investment companies registered as Industrial and Provident Societies and, many of them, soliciting
subscriptions by methods which, besides being illegal under
the Company Act of 1929, would be scorned by coöperative
societies. The appeals of such companies are based upon the
offer of higher rates of interest than can be obtained from
good-class building societies and the safety afforded by investments alleged to be secured on carefully selected real
property. Balance-sheet information, when it is available,
seldom reveals the exact nature of the securities for shares
offered for public subscription; they may be "no more than

a junior mortgage on property already heavily encumbered."[4] Exploiting the impression created by anticoöperative newspapers that coöperative societies do not pay income tax, these property companies claim that the investors' dividends are "free of tax." The *Times*, which speaks on such matters with the authority of the Bank of England, has taken up cudgels against financiers who refuse to play the skin game in accordance with Throgmorton Street rules, and reform of the Industrial and Provident Societies Act is certain, although not in the direction desired by coöperators. Meantime, coöperators may find comfort and amusement in the fact that the *Times*, advocate of penal taxation of coöperative funds, has pronounced the last word on that question in support of its present campaign thus: "It is true that these societies can distribute dividend [i.e., interest on capital] without deductions of income tax, but the dividends form part of the members' taxable income."

Even more vital to the Coöperative Movement are the enactments of Government and those administrative activities of Government departments which ignore the position Coöperation has won in the modern state and impose grave legal limitations on coöperative progress.

Under the Local Government Act of 1933, a member of a local authority having a pecuniary interest in any contract must disclose the fact and refrain from taking part in "the consideration or discussion of or any question with respect to the contract or other matter." This application of a principle of Company Law to public affairs has been interpreted as meaning that a member of a coöperative society serving on a local authority may not vote on bids submitted by his own society or even by a federal society with which his own society is associated. The attitude of the Coöperative Union, upheld by eminent counsel, is that a member or the wife of a member or an employee of a retail distributive society is not disqualified from speaking or voting upon a bid made by a federal

4. *Times*, Nov. 7, 1936.

society, such as a federal dairy, or the C.W.S. This view, in spite of special conditions in the Act to meet such contingencies, has been contested with much vigor. Thus the farcical situation has arisen that private traders may support private enterprise, but coöperators may not support coöperative enterprise and, in local authorities containing a majority of coöperators, it has been impossible to obtain a quorum to begin the business of the authority! Sir Fred Hayward (chairman of the Central Board of the Coöperative Union) and fifty-five of his fellow councilors of Stoke-on-Trent have obtained from the Minister of Health a special dispensation under which an important contract was voted to Burslem and District Coöperative Society. This case has created an important precedent; but it seems reasonable to suggest that steps might have been taken to avoid the necessity for any exercise of ministerial patronage.

When, following the General Strike of 1926, thousands of members of coöperative societies were obliged to apply for public relief, many local authorities resorted to the grossly unfair practices obtaining in the administration of War Relief Funds and insisted that such applicants should withdraw their capital in coöperative societies and that the dividend paid upon their coöperative purchases should be offset against the relief granted. The loss of capital, although large in volume, had no ill effect on societies. Members seeking relief, however, were made to feel that there was no advantage in coöperative trading and that, by withdrawing from coöperative membership, they would be spared some part of the inquisition to which the poor on public funds are subjected. Incidentally, the auditors of the Ministry of Health insisted that dividends on relief vouchers should be paid to the local authorities and not to the individual coöperator, but when private business offered discount or rebates such inducements were treated as a trade expense and not on equal terms with dividends.

Unless a coöperative society owning a chemist's shop elects

the superintending chemist to its committee of management
—a practice which undermines the "Civil Service" status of
the coöperative official—it cannot, under the Poisons and
Pharmacy Acts of 1908 and 1933, describe these shops under
the title of "chemist and druggist," or "chemist or druggist,"
or "dispensing chemist or druggist." More onerous has been
the effect of regulations made by the Ministry of Health,
after consultation with the Retail Pharmacists' Union, preventing coöperative societies from paying dividends on National Health Insurance prescriptions dispensed in their
shops. When a Labor Minister of Health decided to amend
these regulations, action was taken in the courts to restrain
him. The case went to the House of Lords and was decided
in favor of the Minister. Meantime, the Labor Government
went out of office and a Conservative Minister, in answer to
a threat that private retail chemists would strike against the
community, declined to amend the regulations. The interests
of private chemists, who are the largest constituents of the
price-fixing Proprietary Articles Trade Association, are obvious. They resent the capture of a lucrative trade by their
coöperative competitors. They also fear that, if coöperative
societies can return dividends on prescriptions paid for out
of public funds, an inquiring Minister of Health might won-
der if private traders are charging too much!

Eternal vigilance has been the price of freedom to develop
coöperative architectural and also optical services which have
been made subject to regulations akin to the Poisons and
Pharmacy Acts. Political action has had to be taken even to
enable coöperative societies, pioneering the principle of superannuation for employees, to invest the trust funds, now totaling some millions of pounds, within the Coöperative Movement.

Local authorities building new housing estates are zoning
shops and determining whether they will be speciality shops
or general stores. Complaints about discrimination against
coöperative societies are heard in many parts of the country.

Where societies do obtain sites, the range of commodities they supply is determined, not by the demands of their customers, but by the conditions upon which other sites are let to their competitors. To sell chocolates or cigarettes in a general coöperative store would be an offense against the contract between the local authority and the confectioner or tobacconist next door, and is prohibited!

Industry, commerce and finance are being concentrated by the trustification of business and canalized by enactment. Outside the Coöperative Movement the dictation of the money power is triumphant and its triumph is being legalized by Acts of Parliament, frequently at the expense of efficiency. In the notoriously inefficient coal trade, new enterprise is restricted and experiment is frustrated. Owning a modern but partially developed colliery, the C.W.S. must produce only the quota of coal allotted it under the Coal Mines Act or engage in the ridiculous system of buying and selling quotas at monopoly prices, to the detriment of the industry and the community. If a group of railway clerks are thrown out of work by a robot calculator they cannot put a truck on the roads without a license from a Traffic Commissioner, and they will find their application opposed by skilled lawyers on behalf of the railway companies. If a coöperative society decides to provide a road service for its members, it meets the same taboos, and if it obtains a license it will not be permitted to pay dividends to the users of its motor coaches. Laissez faire no longer produces profits. Laissez faire is contrary to the law.

For the free, expanding democracy of Coöperation, the immediate prospect is this: it will secure the place in industry it earns in competition with its rivals in trade and finance, in the Press, and in Parliament.

X.

Growing Pains

GREAT BRITAIN'S ninety-three-year-old Coöperative Movement is still young. Almost alone in an economic system suffering many of the pangs of decay, its afflictions are the pains of growth. Efforts to restrict its expansion have failed. Forecasts setting bounds to its achievements have been falsified. Less than a decade ago some leading coöperators were inclined to cry, "consolidate," and were preaching the doctrine that, in coöperative production at least, the limit had been reached. But enterprise is no less an effect than a cause of growth. From the now powerful distributive societies with large memberships in the great cities, and from the two Wholesale Federations there has come stronger, better directed business leadership during the last ten years. Everywhere, the executive ability which is nurtured slowly in the day-to-day experience of a new type of organization has revealed itself as a challenge to complacency. The Coöperative Movement has become conscious of its national stature, has begun to "think in oceans." Its active membership, subjecting their Movement to a barrage of self-criticisms in hundreds of debates and discussions every week, are learning the lesson of one of their wisest teachers, that whereas "industrial combination is a force, Coöperation is an idea."[1] Its business executives are hammering out the technique for solving the Movement's age-old problem.

Aggregate trade returns are one sign of progress. Average purchases per member are another. Although aggregate coöperative trade and membership have been soaring, a decline in purchases per member has given rise to anxiety. In 1914 sales average per member per week was 11s. 1d. In 1920 it

1. C. R. Fay, *Coöperation at Home and Abroad.*

reached a peak figure of 21*s*. 8*d*. then fell to 13*s*. in 1930, and to 11*s*. in 1934, despite an all round increase in commodity prices between 1914 and 1934 and a vast widening of the range of the coöperative services and facilities.

The figures, of course, must not be accepted at their face value. They are subject to many qualifications.

Between 1921 and 1931, the population of Great Britain grew by 2,600,000, but upon this natural growth there was superimposed a trend from North to South influencing coöperative business probably more than any other business. In Scotland, the Northeast of England and Lancashire and Yorkshire, where Coöperation had its historical roots, natural growth was negatived. Lancashire, indeed, shows an actual decline in population since 1931. Leicestershire, Nottinghamshire and Warwickshire where, outside the more important areas, Coöperation still has to create the fine traditions of the North, all experienced an influx of population. In London and the Southeast, almost a "coöperative desert" as late as 1921, the influx was sufficient to double natural growth. In the Midlands and South, coöperative societies grasped with both hands the opportunity offered them. Coöperative membership in Scotland, for example, rose from 660,000 in 1921 to 760,000 in 1931. Over that same period membership in the Midlands Section of the Coöperative Union rose from 600,000 to 950,000 and in the Southern Section from 670,000 to 1,500,000. The largest retail society in 1914 was Leeds, Yorkshire, with 48,000 members. At the end of 1935, Leeds held sixth place with 115,000 members, being headed by three societies in the South and one in the Midlands.

Important economic consequences followed the trek to the South. Mass markets followed population from the North where the stain of unemployment and poverty, besides becoming permanent, reduced spending power and raised the proportion of the family income paid in local rates. Coöperators moving southward found heavier demands on their income for rent and traveling, fiercer competition for their purchasing loyalty (sometimes in village areas as yet unpenetrated by coöperative enterprise) and a wider variety of nonessential services and entertainment affecting the family budget. Over the whole country, too, business became subject to new dislocations and fluctuations. There was the unevenly distributed but colossal rise in unemployment. There were wage cuts amounting to hundreds of thousands of pounds sterling per week. There was a lowering of income tax exemption limits, and a rise in the rate of taxation. Heavier domestic burdens were offset to a small extent by a fall in prices, but the price level turned sharply upward in 1934. Since 1933, when the Government removed many of the remaining restrictions placed upon the power of property owners to raise house rents, falling incomes have borne a bigger rent charge, and social investigation indicates that rising rents and rates have been paid at the expense of food consumption, especially among the poor. Meanwhile, the rapid spread of home ownership, fostered in the beginning by State subsidy, had stimulated a growing demand for speciality goods in the provision of which coöperators tended to follow rather than to "force" the market.

Two factors peculiar to coöperative development must be observed. Prior to the War, many societies accepted only one person per family, either husband or wife, into membership. Having won from the State the same rights of citizenship accorded them by the Coöperative Movement, housewives induced the majority of societies to adopt the principle of dual membership. There may now be two or more coöperative members in one family with purchases, formerly concentrated in one share number, spread over several share numbers. Again, membership campaigns, especially in the North, have brought people with lower incomes within the circle of coöperators and made loyalty to the coöperative store more extensive than intensive.

In the light of these considerations pessimism is unjusti-

fied. When it is remembered that coöperative retail sales rose
substantially by value between 1924 and 1934—from £175,-
000,000 to £207,000,000—and, since that was a period of
falling prices, sales rose even more substantially by volume,
pessimism is put to rout. The plain fact is that Coöperation
is capturing an ever-growing proportion of the nation's retail trade. In 1934, an index figure of coöperative retail
prices was introduced. Taking that year as 100, 1935 retail
sales rose by 6.5 per cent against a price rise of 4.2 per cent;
a clear increase in volume of 2.3 per cent and, incidentally,
an increase to 11s. 3d. in average sales per member per week.
Under the stimulus of the Ten-Year Plan this process will
be accelerated. Expansion has not been achieved at the expense of financial stability. Between 1914 and 1924, reserve
funds, expressed as a percentage of share capital, fell from
7.3 to 6.8, but between 1924 and 1934 they rose to 9.3.

Nevertheless, the importance of the conclusions drawn by
coöperators from the facile comparison of average sales per
member have had far-reaching effects. There has been an
insistent demand for more, and more reliable, statistics. An
enthusiasm for economic investigation has produced, among
many valuable results, closer collaboration between the
wholesale societies and the Coöperative Union on the one
hand, and between the wholesale societies and their retail
constituents on the other. More particularly, retail societies
themselves have examined price policy and the problems of
relating and amalgamating their activities to secure higher
standards of service and efficiency. In Scotland a strong trend
toward reducing dividends and lowering prices was followed
by an amazing improvement in sales. Liverpool Society, in
1929, began to examine the purchasing records of members.
A test of the trade of 251 persons who had joined the Society
in one week indicated that after ten weeks, 38 had ceased to
purchase. They had drifted away either because they could
not obtain private manufacturers' goods previously bought,
or they found it difficult to habituate themselves to receiving

purchasing vouchers and handling share books, or they could
not obtain weekly credit as hitherto, or they had been wooed
back by their former shopkeepers. Complaints about price
and quality were few. The simple fact was that coöperators
were not telling the story of Coöperation with sufficient
clarity, punch and frequency. A canvassing corps, keeping in
touch with such members and smoothing out the little difficulties arising in early contact with the store, regained for
the society trade amounting to £800 per week during its first
three months of operation. All over the country similar experiments disclosed the need for better publicity and sounder
salesmanship.

Protection of the consumer is the fundamental interest of
coöperators. Today it is being pursued so vigorously as to
have caused what amounts to a reorientation of coöperative
problems and a new approach to their solution.

Consider price policy. Where a society dominates the local
market and pursues a high price and dividend policy, it enables its private trade rivals to exploit the noncoöperative
consumer. High dividends, too, offer little attraction to the
poor whose main aim is to buy cheap; in relation to a society's
overhead charges, they may be conducive to inefficiency.
These are the local aspects of the question. Its national aspects are not less important. If the high-price policy of a
retail coöperative society enables a multiple firm to over-
charge in one town, the society may be subsidizing a multiple attack, through price cutting, on a comrade society in
another town. Of the commodities stocked by a retail society,
perhaps one in every three will be the product of a private
manufacturer and bear a fixed price. Inevitably, the incidence
of high and varying prices falls mostly upon coöperative productions with serious reactions upon the coöperative federations in which the bulk of the retail societies' capital is
invested. When these circumstances obtain, productive federations do not enjoy the full benefit of the retail societies'
organized market. They are obstructed in attempts to increase

their own and the societies' trade by national advertising, since effective advertising requires a clear statement of price.

Here is the case for price fixing by national federations in consultation with the retail societies. A tentative approach to coöperative price fixing over a growing range of commodities has revealed great possibilities. The packaging of the products has been improved. The quality of the publicity placed behind them has become more distinctive. As prices have become standardized, dividends, too, have tended to become uniform, and the problem of "competition" between retail societies serving adjacent and overlapping areas has become more tractable. If coöperators have been habituated to lower dividends, they also have come to expect better service from their own stores. This growth of consumer's confidence has made its own contribution to the recent growth in coöperative trade. Sales per member are still highest where dividends are highest; but it is also true—and the fact is being underlined by experience—that trade and membership are rising most rapidly where dividends and prices are lowest.

Until recent years propaganda for amalgamation between retail societies postulated consolidation as an aim in itself. The present-day slogan is the more encouraging and constructive one of correlation for expansion. It is offensive to coöperators that there should be areas where the Movement places no check upon private business and from which it draws no sustenance. It is equally offensive that societies should continue to offer restricted facilities to members. Thus, while the progress of amalgamation is slow, owing to the democratic, autonomous nature of store organization, there has been a wide expansion of federal dairies, laundries and bakeries and of interesting experiments in fixing maximum dividends by societies in contiguous areas. There has also been a lively willingness to permit the Wholesale Federations to place retail stores in "coöperative deserts," and an encouraging collaboration between groups of retail societies and the Wholesale Federations in the conduct of speciality shops, like druggists and fancy goods bazaars. Some of these schemes are still in embryo. Others have not been in operation long enough to justify an opinion upon their efficacy. What is certain is that the "increments of association" are being utilized by coöperators to make their Movement at once more competitive in the battle for trade and more comprehensive in its service to the general body of consumers.

Not so long ago, the sudden upsurge of gigantic retail societies was thought to be presenting the Movement with new difficulties. Experience suggested that retail societies with memberships between 10,000 and 20,000 represented the ideal units. Such societies did not worship size for the sake of size. There was little danger that organization would not keep pace with growth. Powerful enough to cater to changes in public taste, these societies were not too vast to be capable of comprehension by the ordinary coöperator. It was argued, too, that big societies might well destroy the federal principle. They could buy in sufficient bulk to obtain many of the economies secured by centralized buying through a federation. Tempted by command over a mass market, they might enter into production, perhaps in opposition to their own federations; and, indeed, this fear seemed to be well founded. Several societies, having discovered that the incidence of death among their members was no higher or lower than the average death rate upon which the C.I.S. administered collective life insurance, withdrew from the national scheme and financed their own local schemes. Consciousness of the Movement's national stature eased this problem. Large societies like London (with 575,000 members in 1935), Royal Arsenal (320,000), Birmingham (193,000), South Suburban (150,-000), Liverpool (125,000), Leeds (115,000), Barnsley (91,000), St. Cuthbert's, Edinburgh (80,000), Plymouth (78,000), and Manchester and Salford (77,000) and the twelve others with memberships in excess of 50,000 have, in practice, assumed leadership of the Movement in the drive toward better and bigger production from, and more inten-

sive loyalty to, national federations. Opinion in these societies is backed by economic power. They are at the heart of
the fight for trade and are acutely sensitive to the desires of
the consumer. The national federations must meet their requirements on quality and price. Besides facing realistically
such national coöperative questions as the taking of political
action and the building of a Coöperative Press, the effects of
the insistence of the large societies on better business has been
to brace the entire Movement to that vigorous action which
successful example can best inspire. Nowhere are the possibilities of coöperative expansion revealed more clearly than
in the large retail societies providing an all-inclusive consumer service from a baby shop to a funeral furnishing and
undertaking department. The Royal Arsenal Society, for instance, has found that, given more trade in its funeral department, it can carry the cost of extending collective life
insurance to cover the children of its members. Its collective
insurance scheme has been so extended with the added proviso that, before the member realizes its cash value, the cost
of the burial undertaken by the Society is deducted. Besides
covering life insurance, the scheme now assumes the aspect
of burial benefit. The Society develops a new service for a
certain market. The member is relieved of a charge designed
to provide for burial costs which appears in the majority of
working-class budgets. For the retail coöperative society and
the individual member there are positive gains. For the whole
Movement there is opened up the prospect of a complete co-
operative funeral undertaking service whether organized by
local or national federations.

The value of this type of experiment is beyond estimate.
Coöperators can and do exercise considerable control over
retail prices. Until that control, by virtue of direct coöperative production, covers wholesale prices and productive costs,
the protection afforded the consumer by Coöperation will
remain imperfect. In the coöperative business world, as elsewhere, there is a natural resistance to production by the

Movement of commodities already dominated by private manufacture. The manager of a coöperative factory will be enthusiastic about expanding the output of his plant. The buyer in a coöperative warehouse, however great his coöperative integrity, may be reluctant to restrict his purchases to one manufacturer, since his efficiency is measured by sales volume. This reluctance may be shared by retail managers and shop assistants animated more by anxiety to give the consumer what he wants than by the idea of directing consumers' wants into coöperative channels. Here are problems of the technical and coöperative education of employees which the larger societies, in conjunction with the national federations and the Coöperative Union, have been foremost in tackling.

Hitherto, the production and sale of motor cars and similar articles, now "improvement-of-living" goods and not mere luxuries, have been regarded outside the sphere of coöperative enterprise. The C.W.S. does a flourishing trade in building motor bodies. National federations are looking sympathetically to American coöperative oil refineries for petrol supplies. The C.I.S. captures a growing proportion of motor insurance business. A way of filling in the blanks will become imperative as each of these existing forms of enterprise expands, and the success of the application of mass production methods in coöperative factories in recent years suggests that the barriers in the way are not insurmountable. A breach has been made by the C.W.S. in the virtual monopoly of Great Britain's bicycle trade by two private combines, and coöperative cycles and motor cycles are on the road. Many retail societies conduct excursion and travel departments. Between the two services is the difference of catering to mass demand and to more or less individual taste. It is a difference which many forward-looking coöperators would like to bridge.

The heart and brain of the entire Movement is the Coöperative Union. In Great Britain, the Coöperative Union is an *ad hoc* body, separated from the trading units of the Move-

A modern department store in a London suburb

Shornells, Abbey Wood, London recreational and educational center of the Royal Arsenal Coöperative Society ment and binding them only by links of loyalty to coöperative ideals. This ad hoc position, once a weakness of the Coöperative Movement, is now a source of strength. Until the Wholesale Federations played a full part in the work of the Union, counsels were divided and Coöperation lacked an authoritative voice. What the annual congress of the Union decided was not necessarily endorsed by the quarterly meeting of the C.W.S., and coöperative committeemen listened to the opinion of the businessmen more gladly than they heard the pronouncements of the propagandists. The division was irksome and inherently dangerous. Today, as they help to shape the policy of the Coöperative Union, the trading federations accept full responsibility for giving effect to the Union's decisions and the Movement is more united than ever before in its history. One result is a vast improvement in research work, in the application of research service to every aspect of coöperative trade, propaganda and education. Few questions can arise in coöperative board rooms, whether of stock control, bookkeeping, the organization of welfare work among employees or the better use of display material, to which the headquarters' staff of the Coöperative Union cannot provide the answer, and the daily task of the Union is the promotion of better coöperative business. Standardization of retail bookkeeping, for example, provides coöperative federations with detailed information that can be used to rectify errors and waste, and reduce excessive overhead charges caused by the carrying of too large a stock and faulty distribution of work. Refusal to obey the Union is not unknown. Occasionally a Labor conciliation award, made under Union auspices, is scorned by a local committee of management, or a recommendation for amalgamation between two societies is rejected. Coöperators are human beings and their institutions reflect human frailties. Yet Coöperation is a Movement. It is not a mob. The desire to act in unison is deeply rooted in the fact that, thanks largely to the work of the Union, coöperators think in unison. Occasionally an impatient note, which every progressive mind in the Movement must echo, is struck in pleas for the endowment of the Union with compulsory powers. It is not inconceivable that the Union will obtain such powers by consent of its constituents. It cannot assume them. But the overriding question is this: how soon, under the pressure of events, and how far, under the wise tuition of the Union itself, will retail societies agree to the coöperative nationalization of many of their trading services while retaining their own local character? This local character is of the essence of coöperative democracy and is precious to British coöperators. Its suppression would be harmful ethically. It might even be unsound economically.

Already the Coöperative Movement has revealed itself as responsive to the cry for rationalization in a manner guaranteeing efficiency to the consumer without imposing expensive superstructures on trade and commerce. Side by side with improvements in the internal working of each of the constituent units, there have marched more imaginative measures of coordination between the separate units. As the Economic Consultative Committee of the League of Nations observed in 1929, "the peculiar feature of co-operative vertical combination is that it groups economic units which are both very numerous and very small, urban and rural households, peasant holdings and small craft undertakings. . . . When the English C.W.S. obtains supplies of raw materials for its soap factory from its own palm groves," the report continues, "this vertical combination towards the source of supplies is based ultimately on the four million households which are united in the twelve hundred societies forming the English Wholesale Society. In the same way the Danish Co-operative Trading Company, which is the most important organisation for the distribution of bacon in Great Britain, is composed of eighteen Danish co-operative slaughter houses which in turn are based on the association of more than 85 per cent of the Danish peasants. The latter are, however, organised in other specialised systems for the requirements of their holdings or their households . . . while vertical combination as usually described seems to apply only to those branches of the economic system in which large scale undertakings predominate and particularly to large industrial undertakings, the co-operative movement succeeds in achieving the technical and economic organisation of innumerable units of the agricultural, craft and household system. Co-operative vertical combination thus makes possible and carries out for the benefit of small units all the measures of simplification and reduction of costs to which every scheme of this kind leads . . . the opportunity for this economy at the basis of the system arises from the relations of the primary society with its own members . . ."[2]

From this stimulating generalization there emerges another: that, except in isolated instances, the existence of a small coöperative society in the retail market may be as natural and can be as economic as the existence of a large coöperative society. There follows the conclusion, also noted in the report quoted, that the proper task of consumer coöperative societies is to expand their known market by expanding and making constant the purchases of their members, and to secure from their membership active participation in the adoption of measures intended to reduce expenses and increase the efficiency of the system in general.

It is also as clear as daylight that the present will not be the final stage of British retail trade. "Distribution costs are a far heavier burden than society permanently will consent to bear." The nation will not tolerate permanently a system which does not deliver the goods the consumer wants of a quality he wants in the place where he wants them. The awakening of the consumer implies the existence of a medium through which awareness can find expression. That medium is the democratic, autonomous retail coöperative society, be it large or small.

2. Preliminary Note on Rationalization and Labor Conditions, April 23, 1929.

Whether a movement composed of many constituents can respond quickly and enthusiastically to national leadership depends, as the success of the Ten-Year Plan shows, on the quality of the leadership. The progress of that plan will continue to derive from the quality of its leadership. Its first impulse has been toward increasing coöperative trade and membership. It may be directed as easily toward intensifying the purchasing loyalty of coöperators, raising the average sales per member per week, or expanding existing services and developing new ones. It can raise the demand for coöperative productions, sustain a campaign for consumers' education, open up countless possibilities of winning all Britain to the principles and practice of Coöperation. It is axiomatic, however, that every direction of the plan must be chosen with care and only after examination of the facts of business. To follow some rivals of the Coöperative Movement in forcing markets that are spurious, to stimulate tastes that are transient for the purpose of speculative investment would be foolish and uncharacteristic of Coöperation, which has a continuous life based upon responsibility to the community.

Coöperative problems are unending. The Coöperative Movement will find in growing pains a permanent affliction; an affliction which only the prescription of "more and more vigorous growth" will alleviate.

XI.

Personal Problems

"A MAN cannot make a pair of boots for a committee," declared Mr. Eric Gill, distinguished typographer, on a famous occasion,[1] neatly begging the question of the right relationship between knowledge and power in the democratic conduct of affairs. The question affects the official, whether of coöperative society or joint-stock company, even more acutely than it affects the artist, for while the latter may retire to his ivory tower, the former is called, perhaps to conflict, in the boardroom. Moreover, the body grows faster than the brain, organization outpaces thought and technique, yet it is only where organization ends that thought begins.

Here is the explanation of many of the personal paradoxes of business life. Wealthy magnates deplore the shortage of men capable of controlling great undertakings. Technicians complain of ignorant, intractable directors, and would welcome statutory assistance to establish a dictatorship of Knowledge over Power. Under pressure of competition, the machinery of far-flung organizations is improvised, the technique of direction is given little chance to mature, the adjustment of duties between men exercising executive power develops too slowly. Big businesses, especially those engaged in public utilities, have endeavored to acquire a Civil Service technique and tradition by recruiting Treasury officials to their staffs. The State itself, however, finds difficulty in commanding ability commensurate with its modern tasks. In the electricity, coal, iron and steel and fishing industries, State-inspired efforts have been made in recent years to replace rugged indi-

1. Mr. Gill was invited to submit to a committee designs for a new type face for a London newspaper.

vidualism by collaboration. Administrators enjoying the confidence of businessmen and endowed with the required *expertise* have been so rare that two or three men have played "general post" between industry and industry. Even lawyers whom governments appoint chairmen of commissions to which are referred thorny questions politicians wish to shelve are few in number. Lord MacMillan, noted public servant, is among the elite. Conservative Lord Advocate for Scotland in the first Labor Government (!) he presided ably over an inquiry into the administration of lunatic asylums, then conducted long investigations into coal, the British Pharmacopoeia, finance and industry, income tax, and wages in the woolen industry. In the middle of this process of being groomed as a more or less permanent economic legal adviser to the State, his lordship is reported to have suggested that he might be given something interesting to investigate, something he could discuss with his wife. He was appointed chairman of a committee inquiring into the night life of London and the habits of the ladies of the town!

Nevertheless, the expert, whether good or bad, is expected to possess some modicum of knowledge; but anybody can be a director and, cried the Senior Official Receiver in 1925, too many directors are "expert in nothing at all."[2]

A director may be chosen by virtue of his ability in accountancy, law, or engineering. He may be selected, especially by a bank, because of his intimacy with its branch customers. He may be expected to introduce business to the company. These tests are being applied more generally now than ever before, but their application is far from being general. Titles retain their snob value in Great Britain. In an analysis of the directorates of one hundred companies, Miller and Campbell[3] found that the proportion of peers and heirs of peers was at least 15.3 per cent and the proportion of names with the prefix "Sir" over 24.3 per cent, a total of nearly 40 per cent. Nepotism determines many directorships. The fact that

2. *Financial Democracy*, p. 71.   3. *Idem*, p. 78 *et seq.*

criticism cannot be urged against a son brought up in the atmosphere of his father's business following his father's footsteps is counterbalanced heavily by the fact that natural young ability unsupported by wealth or influence shuns business and enters the Civil Service and the professions, where it is better rewarded. The one universal test for directors is the share qualification, which might be £100, as in the case of the Marconi Company, or £5,000, as in the case of the Imperial Tobacco Company. What principle governs such a test? The £100 qualification can be satisfied by almost anybody. The other cannot be satisfied by any nobody.

The test for directors of a coöperative society, although incapable of application in capitalist industry, does satisfy a simple principle, for it requires a prior interest by the aspiring director in the affairs of the business. It is a capital ownership and purchasing test, fixed so low that it presents no obstacle to the very poor man, but high enough to insure that he has first-hand knowledge of the society's services. While it is obvious that a meeting of coöperative shareholders is unlikely to elect a director because of his special knowledge, membership in the society implies local knowledge on the part of the candidate and, on the part of the electors, knowledge of his integrity. Nepotism is absent in the coöperative directorate. Coöperative directors have no hereditary rights. Several men have been awarded knighthoods because of service to the community through the Coöperative Movement. But no man ever became a coöperative director because he sports a title. Knighthoods have no commercial value in nonspeculative business. The progress of the coöperator, as a rule, is through the educational, social or political agencies of the society, and the winning of a reputation on "the floor of the house" of the society's business meeting, to the committee of management. No stranger to a coöperative society's business meeting can expect to leap from orchestra to footlights at one bound. Experience of educational administration does not convert a bricklayer or cotton operative or brewery clerk into a heaven-sent administrator. It does, however, habituate him to the routine of committee work and the discipline of committee debate. Once on a committee of management, the director must serve a period of apprenticeship before being eligible for nomination to the directorate of a local or national federation. The local retail society is a training ground from which the National Movement draws administrators already skilled in coöperative business.

Directors' fees vary in commerce. They are seldom high enough to justify an able man in making a profession of directorships, although they may be high enough to attract the "guinea pig."[4] Their cost, measured in relation to every £100 of issued capital, ranges from 2d. (a far from typical low level; 1s. 2d. is more typical) to 11s. 7d. and averages 2s. 6d.[5] This is not a burdensome charge. It is sufficiently low to enable directors to evade responsibility—"if you have a company with fifteen directors and pay them £200 per year each, you cannot expect them to sit in the office five days a week, and you cannot even expect them to attend every meeting"[6] —and it is sufficiently low to encourage pluralism among "guinea pigs." Yet it is high compared with the similar costs of coöperative administration. These average, probably, less than ½d. per £100 of capital in retail societies where, directorial service being voluntary, costs are covered in a series of small honoraria fixed by rule, and less than 1d. in the C.W.S. with twenty-eight full-time directors. Occasionally coöperators indulge in heart searching on the question of appointing and paying full-time directors. But Coöperation is not a career; it is the commercial expression of a cause; and voluntary directorships are of the spirit of voluntary Coöperation. No body of coöperative shareholders would elect a man a full-time director, taking him from his every-

4. Contemptuous term for one who receives a fee of a guinea.
5. *Financial Democracy*, p. 81.
6. A. F. Topham, K.C., in evidence before Company Law Amendment Committee. *Financial Democracy*, p. 81.

day employment, then reject him lightly when he presented himself for reëlection. Again, a full-time director in daily contact with shareholders who exercise greater vigilance than similar groups of joint-stock company shareholders must be possessed of more than average courage to pursue a policy which may be unpalatable to a section of the members who can make their opposition felt by attacking him in a position involving his livelihood. Circumstances alter cases. The needs of the larger society may require the election of full-time directors—the C.W.S. could not be administered well by part-time directors—but in the main the voluntary system is an assurance of integrity in the Coöperative Movement and it does not endanger efficiency where voluntary directors realize that direction of policy and not the performance of executive duties is their job.

If Coöperation demands no specialized knowledge from those aspiring to its directorates, it does succeed in utilizing specialized knowledge in its directorships. A coöperative manager may not be elected a director of the society employing him but, having won the confidence of the members of his own and neighboring societies, he may be elected a director of a federation of societies.

The present chairman of the C.W.S., Mr. William Bradshaw, is a case in point. The son of a Derbyshire miner, he became a coöperative messenger boy at the age of thirteen and in turn grocery apprentice, shop assistant and manager of a small coöperative society. In 1903, at the age of twenty-six, he was appointed general manager and secretary of the Grantham Coöperative Society, then in the throes of financial crisis. In thirteen short years he had nursed the Society to a position of strength and stability and been made the recipient of high public honors. Active in the professional organization of coöperative officials, Mr. Bradshaw did much to raise their status. During the Great War, he was a coöperative representative on Ministry of Food committees and a member of the Food Control Committee. With his election to the directorate of the C.W.S. came opportunities of travel in more than twenty countries, first-hand study of the problems of international trade and exchange and intimate contact with coöperative production. No better training for his present onerous post could be imagined. Mr. Bradshaw is the first manager of a coöperative retail society to be elected president of the C.W.S., but many coöperative employees and officials, by virtue of their enthusiasm for the cause of Coöperation and their competence in its commercial practice, have found that they carry the coöperative equivalent of a marshal's baton in their knapsacks. Of the present twenty-eight C.W.S. directors, twelve were formerly officials of retail societies, two were employed by the Coöperative Union and one by the C.W.S. itself, and thirteen were either presidents or members of the boards of management of retail societies. Mr. Neil S. Beaton, the colorful chairman of the Scottish C.W.S., was formerly a shop assistant, trade union organizer, S.C.W.S. traveling propagandist (to him goes much of the credit for the development of retail coöperative societies in the Highlands of Scotland) and S.C.W.S. director. Five of the twelve Scottish directors were employees of the Movement prior to their election to the Board, the other seven being chairmen of smaller federal bodies or retail societies.

These facts suggest that, spontaneously, coöperators are achieving an effective balance between knowledge, enjoying the privilege of winning the ear of the masses, and power which has been wise enough to fit itself by study of business technique.

Pluralism and the rule of the aged are two of the curses implicit in joint-stock companies of which anybody can become a director. The Railway Clerks' Association drew public attention to the existence, in 1929, of eighty-two railway directors who held between them 596 directorships, so that they could not be single minded and "solely devoted to the transport service"; and there is general endorsement of the view that, while the varying energies and abilities of men are not susceptible of statistical analysis, it is impossible to regard the diversion of one man's attention over fifty companies as being in the interests of the community. From an examination of a sample of 30,000 directors in 1932[7] it appears that the vast majority (90 per cent) hold less than five director-ships, 7.4 per cent hold between five and nine, 1.4 per cent between ten and fourteen, .6 per cent between fifteen and nineteen, and .5 per cent more than twenty directorships. The pluralists with fifty directorships form a negligible group and are accounted for mainly by subsidiaries. But the pluralists holding directorships in excess of five control the major part of British industry. They form, write Miller and Campbell, "that nebulous body the 'College of Directors'—possibly one or two thousand in number—who provide the nucleus of the Boards of the majority of the big industrial concerns, and who, even though having some outsiders as colleagues, can, by their very prestige and plurality of office, wield an in-fluence out of proportion to their numbers." And they include a large proportion of those titled gentry who might be de-scribed fairly as "guinea pigs."

Age levels have been influenced by the Great War. Men who would be now in the prime of business life and vigor were lost to the nation. However we regard the merits of the controversy between youth and crabbed age, which the State seems to have decided by allowing special income-tax relief after the age of 65 because the taxpayer is "old and infirm," the places of Great Britain's lost youth have not been filled by the young. They have been held by the old. In a 77 per cent sample of the directors of one hundred British companies controlling in 1932 £2,050,000,000 of capital, Miller and Campbell found 30.3 per cent of directors aged between 61 and 70 and 26.7 per cent over 70. Few were below 45. A mere handful were below 40 and of these the overwhelming majority were either "sons of their fathers" or had started commercial life with the advantages of wealth and position.

7. *Financial Democracy*, p. 107.

The average age was 63.[8] In the Coöperative Movement, many retail societies compel retirement from committees of management at 65. The two Wholesale Federations super-annuate directors at 68 and the average age of their directors in August, 1936, was 49 in England (where no person over 50 is eligible for nomination) and 58 in Scotland.

The structure of the Coöperative Movement lends itself to a peculiar form of pluralism. A retail society director may be elected a director of a federal laundry or bakery. Sometimes he will be called upon to resign his retail directorship. Always the natural keenness of his colleagues themselves to serve on federal organizations will limit his pluralism. Retail societies, however, regard representation on national federations as an honor. In search of honor, unless their rules specifically prohibit them, they may propose their best-known director for election to several federations. Thus one man, director of a retail society, may sit also on the committee of a local federal body and a sectional board of the Coöperative Union, may be elected to subcommittees of the national organizations of these local units, and may find his time fully occupied by a multiplicity of committee duties. Here, again, exercise of the art of delegation of task is of major importance. The alternative is the creation of a hierarchy which must fail to function.

Since a trained coöperative official may take his place as an elected person on coöperative federations—Sir Fred Hayward, chairman of the Central Board of the Coöperative Union, was managing secretary of Burslem and District Coöperative Society and was as distinguished in his business capacity as he is now popular in the role of leader—the coöperative expert is always on tap although never on top. In the very act of bringing business administration into conformity with democratic principles he influences policy and enjoys a privilege of which most technicians only dream. Enthusiasm and enterprise spring rather from the substance

8. *Financial Democracy*, p. 93.

than from the form of democracy. A hierarchy of officials, buttressed in their position by organization and procedure which bring their executive activities under periodical review by committeemen is conceivable and has worked successfully in some of the European movements which worship at the shrine of Rochdale. But the men of Rochdale sought something more than satisfaction for urgent economic needs. They sought self-expression for their genius for self-government, and self-government is part of the tradition of British Coöperation. In a Movement that remains true to tradition, problems of *expertise* cannot be solved by definition of the administrative duties of business executives. Definition derives from practice; and coöperative practice can be influenced most speedily by the character and quality of officials themselves.

A cause of lively speculation among outside observers of the Coöperative Movement is the relationship between committeemen earning low wages in private employment and officers paid munificent salaries. The outsider is surprised to learn that a business turning over hundreds of millions of pounds sterling per annum and paying its rank and file generously has no £10,000-a-year men, no £5,000-a-year men, very few £2,000-a-year men, and only a tiny minority of executives in receipt of upward of £1,000 a year. No coöperative official receives from the Movement what is called a "commercial salary." Yet few are attracted to competitive business though many are tempted. The reason is that Coöperation, like public office, is a service and, from the viewpoint of the official who has grown up in the coöperative tradition, an honorable service. Such men, now numbering 7,000, crave status, opportunity for initiative and the right to walk with dignity. How status has been won in practice is well illustrated in the story of the official body of coöperative executives, the National Coöperative Managers' Association and the Coöperative Secretaries' Association, whose memberships are combined in the National Union of Coöperative

Officials. These professional associations have improved and unified conditions of service. They have promoted the efficiency of their own members. They are numbered among those voluntary organizations of experts which, like the Engineering Standards Committee, lack legislative or other authority, yet have caused manufacturers in many fields to feel constrained to make use of specific material of specific shape, size and weight, put together in a specific way, in the words of Mr. and Mrs. Sidney Webb, "by the mere weight of expert agreement." So profound has been "the weight of expert agreement" in coöperative administration that officials enjoy the right, now recognized by all sections of the elected coöperative democracy, to be consulted in formulating national trade and financial policy. They have revealed the "most valuable characteristic of the brain-working professions in Great Britain" by establishing a claim to "intellectual freedom in the exercise of their several functions."

Standardized bookkeeping, the setting up of trade associations now beginning, through the Coöperative Union, to engage in research work, rationalization of coöperative business —all this has grown under the creative impulse of officials who, while actively aware of their responsibility to public opinion represented by the committeeman, have developed an *esprit de corps* of their own. Thus coöperative issues have been sorted out, deëmotionalized and made more tractable, and the quality of coöperative public opinion has been improved. Official thought has been fertilized by contact with the common man and the common man himself has grown in business stature. Coöperation has still to discover in detail the right relationship between democracy and the expert. Far from resigning that task, it has brought a major problem of business and politics sufficiently near to solution to encourage the view that coöperative democracy will yet point a way to democratic revival in Great Britain.

XII.

Coöperation and the Standard of Living

ALTHOUGH Coöperation has earned the place it has won in capitalist society, coöperators claim no proprietary rights in progress. Progress in the democratic State is not a private possession. It is a collective heritage. Yet to affirm that Coöperation has enriched the public heritage and contributed substantially toward the social welfare of the British people is to affirm a fact beyond dispute.

Rochdale's Pioneers acted in response to the demand of a poverty-stricken population for some amelioration of the lot which condemned them to hard labor, meager rewards and blind, almost reverential, obedience to man-made economic laws. Rochdale's Pioneers wielded the weapon nearest to their hands. They wielded it with such effect that the consumer found, immediately, a way of escape from the toils of debt to small traders, a way to independence in the exercise of his purchasing loyalty, a way to accumulate capital on his own account and a way to improve his standard of living by the voluntary organization and direction of his economic power. For the coöperator there have been positive benefits in the form of purer food, more economic spending of the family budget, the encouragement of thrift, and participation in business government. The noncoöperator, too, has benefited. For him there has been the protection afforded by the existence of an alternative to private trading, a salutary check upon the abuse of monopoly power and the defeat, in many fields of enterprise, of indifference to the essential interests of the consuming public.

Quality in the goods it supplies is implicit in the coöperative system. It is also fundamental to the success earned by

the Movement in distribution and production; and the
failure of the State to enforce effective food standards has
made pursuit of purity by coöperators more imperative. Testing of raw materials is a managerial function in the coöperative factory. Inspection of the product at every process is a departmental duty. Many societies in the milk trade engage
one skilled analyst to sample milk at the creamery and another to sample it at the retail dairies; and similar care is
exercised throughout the myriad of services. External form
and internal organization may not differentiate the coöperative factory from other large-scale factories any more in this,
the protection of consumers' interests in the quality of the
product offered for sale, than in some other aspects of modern
enterprise. Private companies contribute no less enthusiastically than coöperative societies to voluntary agencies for
consumer research. But these claims can be advanced for Co-
operation: not all private businesses are reputable, and the
consumer research which has been the care of coöperators for
ninety-three years has become the care of the general business
community only within the last two decades.

Is Coöperation maintaining its historical lead in quality?
Comparison is difficult and where it is possible may be influenced as much by political as by other considerations. Contracts to supply hospitals, for obvious reasons, offer one
test. Not all British hospitals, however, are financed from
public funds, and cheapness rather than quality may determine the placing of their contracts. Governors of hospitals
are usually traders in competition with coöperative societies.
In bidding for hospital contracts, coöperative societies frequently find that the specifications permit only the supply
of private makers' brands. One of the biggest hospitals in
Scotland recently freed soap bids from these restrictive stipulations. When the S.C.W.S. beat every competitor on price
a demand for a test on quality was raised and applied. The
S.C.W.S. retained the contract. In another important hospital a contract for fish was withdrawn from a private sup-

plier and a decision taken to buy daily from a coöperative depot at current prices. A rise in the consumption of fish alarmed the governors. The instinctive reaction of some of them, familiar with the methods of less reputable business, was "graft," although, in relation to its trade, the Coöperative Movement lends more support to the Bribery and Secret Commissions Prevention League than any other organization in Great Britain. Investigation revealed that while the fish bill was going up, the bills for other commodities were going down. The hospital's staff, of their own free choice, now considered the fish supply to patients good enough for consumption by themselves. In obtaining hospital contracts coöperative societies must beat their competitors on price. It may be taken for granted that they are required also to beat competitors on quality. The capture of an increasing number of such contracts by the Coöperative Movement is a pointer to the purity of the goods it produces. In defense of its own principles Coöperation has ventured into enterprises like the manufacture of medicines, where State regulation of quality is almost noneffective and voluntary regulation is noninclusive. There is no reason to believe that Coöperation's influence on these productions will not become as potent as it has been in other commodities.

In evidence before the Select Committee on Medicine Stamp Duty Acts on January 25, 1937, a coöperative deputation, claiming to speak for "consumers, wholesale manufacturing chemists, those engaged in retail pharmacy, and also . . . retail grocers," suggested the abolition or reduction of duties upon patent medicines and undertook, if the duties were repealed, to pass on the whole of the benefit to the consumer. The deputation also proposed that "it should be made compulsory for manufacturers to disclose the formula of patent medicines to a responsible body (impartial in its representation and including professional knowledge) before offering the article to the public."[1]

1. *Coöperative News*, January 30, 1937.

Weight and measure are both elements in price. Here
again the record of Coöperation bears strict examination. The
public campaign by which the Coöperative Movement obtained the application of uniform standards to the weight and
packaging of tea has extended to other commodities like coal,
and may be said to be sustained by its normal practice. On
questions of price the evidence of the Movement's success in
safeguarding its own members and of its vigilance in check-
mating, on behalf of the whole community, the moves of
price-for-profit fixers and monopolists is overwhelming.
Then there is the dividend. An addition of £25,000,000 a
year to the purchasing power of the coöperative section of the
community is an assurance of better nutrition and better living for one in every two families in Great Britain. On the
average, the coöperative dividend adds £4 to the annual income of the coöperative family. It provides a sum equal to
one week's pay for the better-off salaried worker and equal
to two weeks' pay for the poorer paid laboring classes.

Every campaign for coöperative trade and membership
widens the area of employment governed by trade union
conditions. The British Movement is the traditional ally of
Trade Unionism, its banker in industrial peace, and its com-
missariat in days of unrest, and coöperative example has been
a powerful lever in the hands of trade unionists for improving labor conditions over great sections of industry. Facing
the same problems of human relations as private business,
the Coöperative Movement, in the words of Professor Clay,
Economic Adviser to the Bank of England, has "to face the
problems of adjusting the conflicting claims of wage earners
who want higher wages and customers who want lower prices
. . . Its business is subject to the dislocating influences of
seasonal change, varying harvest yields, fluctuating prices,
and general trade fluctuations; it cannot, therefore, guarantee
its members against unfavourable price movements or its employees against interruption of employment."[2] As expansion

2. *Coöperation and Private Enterprise*, p. 9.

of their known market enables coöperative societies to insulate their members more and more from unfavorable price movements, so it enables them to insulate employees against "interruption of employment," and the unmistakable responsibility borne by consumers for the wages they pay and the conditions they impose is an assurance against overwork and underpay. Three years before the State made a frontal attack on sweating in selected trades, coöperators, as we have seen, had endorsed and were applying the principle of the minimum wage. Testimony to the value of coöperative effort to promote the welfare of the most helpless and least organized section of work people is clinched by the evidence of Mr. J. Hallsworth, a leader of the National Union of Distributive and Allied Workers. "Public convenience," he writes, "often has been and again may be pleaded as the excuse for the later hours of closing shops and excessive labour of shop assistants . . . In this connection emphasis may be laid on the fact that the co-operative stores throughout the country cater for classes of consumers in respect of which the question of convenience has always required special consideration. It is a striking manifestation of the change of habits on the part of the shopping public that in these stores . . . the hours between which shops are open have been contracted sufficiently to allow within them for a working week of 48 hours down to 44 hours as the maximum. It is true that the minority of shop assistants are engaged in co-operative stores, but it is also true that the geographical distribution of such stores and the classes for which they cater are sufficiently representative of the general conditions as to support fully the contention that what has been achieved by agreement . . . shall be extended to all classes of shops by legislation."[3]

Coöperation has done as much to abolish "the working man" as to elevate him. For forty years before the men of Great Britain won adult male suffrage, and for three quarters of a century before universal suffrage was attained, the Co-

3. *Commercial Employees and Protective Legislation.*

operative Movement endowed every man and woman within its boundaries with every privilege of democracy and equality. Ninety years ago, it was unthinkable that differences in the rewards did not demonstrate also differences in the quality, even in the texture, of human beings. As late as the turn of the present century it was difficult to imagine the laborer as a scholar, or the scholar as the laborer. That compound of fear and envy men then called respect, applied to function as well as to ownership in the capitalist State.

The coöperative boardroom and the coöperative classroom uprooted both types of snobbery, to the great enrichment of the nation. At any given moment, in management committees, educational committees, political societies, men's and women's guilds and a score of other coöperative agencies, there are upwards of 30,000 citizens exercising the arts of government. Familiar with the conduct of business, they are neither palsied by ignorance nor galvanized into irresponsible action when confronted with grave issues. They bridge the gulf between the ideals of the propagandist and the realities of the administrator. They give to the mass of democracy the quality which once was the possession of the few, and citizenship is honored and glorified by their gift.

Coöperative education is vocational. It is also cultural. Great Britain's first free libraries were coöperative libraries. The Coöperative Movement gave birth to the idea and, in conjunction with trade unions and the Working Men's Clubs and Institute Union, sustenance to the organization of the Workers' Educational Association which links the university to the people. In 1904, Reading Coöperative Society united University College with every working-class association in the town in the first W.E.A. branch. Two years later, Rochdale coöperators fostered the first of the university tutorial classes which opened up new avenues of opportunity for serious working men and women students and influenced the progress of adult education all over the English-speaking world.

This pioneer effort to realize an "earth crammed with heaven" goes on and on. Many retail societies and the Coöperative Union smooth the path of scholarship for the children of coöperators through secondary schools to the universities and the Coöperative College. For adults, there is contact with Coöperative Union classes, the Workers' Educational Association, and the National Council of Labor Colleges. Great Britain's amateur dramatic movement owes much to coöperative support, so much that idealists dream of the creation of a coöperative theater. A circuit of seventy coöperative cinemas opens up the possibility of the intelligent consumer's at last being enabled to indicate his preferences in a form of entertainment which confuses box-office receipts with "what the public wants." Choral singing, a natural joy of the inheritors of a lovely language and a rich treasury of folk songs, is fostered by coöperative associations. What thousands of British children know of the folk dance they learn in coöperative junior guilds. All over the country, coöperators initiate and finance social services designed to mitigate the plight of the aged poor (many societies give free bread to aged members), ease the lot of the sick by providing sickroom appliances, secure their own employees against poverty in old age through superannuation schemes, donate generously to the provision of public amenities, and blaze the trail to State assurance of equity for every man.

These are the traditions inspiring coöperators in their untiring work of education and reform, molding their conception of the store in relation to the State and harmonizing their business practices with social ideals.

Yesterday, the coöperators' known market was a theory. Today it is a power. Businessmen, actuated by the profit motive, seek to control a known market by world-wide combination. Governments, in answer to industry's demand for release from the menace of recurring boom and slump, resort to fiscal expedients to regulate and measure markets. Tomorrow, the nation will look beyond coöperative achievement to coöperative methods, will learn this lesson of democracy in business: that the secret of prosperity is to return the economies effected by organization of the market to the consumers composing it, and so to expand the market by raising the standard of living of every man, woman and child. "Broadly speaking," the *Times* assures its readers, "the ratio between profits and wages corresponds with the ratio between immediate consumption and investment for more production," and if industrial expansion is to continue, "every increase in productive powers must be accompanied by a corresponding distribution, either through wages or through the social services, of the means by which it may be bought for consumption."[4] The capitalist's dilemma has never been described more succinctly. The objective that realistic capitalist opinion would win by higher wages, the Coöperative Movement is endeavoring to achieve now by distribution of dividends on purchases.

4. January 22, 1937.

XIII.

A New Voice in Politics

POLITICS is a department of commerce, and the consumer, Forgotten Man of commerce, is also the Forgotten Man of politics. The sheer weight of its wealth and the propaganda power of its newspapers entrench economic autocracy in the councils of political democracy. Day by day, governments render account to representatives of "the Invisible Empire of Big Business," whether on the floor of the House of Commons or in the municipal chamber. Public opinion is articulate enough, but its impact upon the daily administration of public affairs is negligible.

Outraged by wartime profiteering, consumers forced a series of investigations which, between 1918 and 1924, produced a devastating criticism of private enterprise and more or less detailed plans for bringing business practice into conformity with modern ideas. Yet the citadels of economic autocracy remained unshaken. Putting these plans in operation would have required a frontal attack, which Conservative and Liberal statesmen did not dare to undertake, upon vested interests. The inquiry yielded nothing more than a Food Council, able to call but not to compel evidence, and unable to initiate legislation—a mere blanket between Government and consumer. The biggest petition ever presented to any Parliament did not prevent the imposition of additional taxation upon coöperative funds by the first National Government. Of the 615 members of that Parliament, the majority were landowners, industrialists, financiers or lawyers, 190 of whom held 700 directorships in food firms, distributing combines, drapery houses, insurance companies and other businesses in active trading competition with the Coöperative Movement.

The businessman in politics is not oblivious to the public good. He is the exponent of what might have been good for the public a hundred years ago. Well served in his private life by the intellectual superstitions which nineteenth-century philosophers sanctified as "economic laws," he relates the public good to the individual, sectional interests with which he is most familiar, and the case of the consumer, because of its general nature, goes by default. The spirit of the section is everywhere rampant—"the defiant fragment claiming to act as if it were the whole"[1]—and the preferences of unorganized consumers have even less influence upon politics than upon production and distribution.

As long ago as 1902 coöperators had learned the lesson that, in capitalist society, political action is dictated by economic power. They then created a Joint-Parliamentary Committee of the Coöperative Congress to protect their general interests against "the defiant fragment." Ten years later, William Maxwell urged Congress to effect a fusion of forces between the Coöperative, Trade Union and Labor Movements not to bring politics into Coöperation but to take Coöperation into politics. In 1917, flouted by governments and persecuted by trade rivals enjoying political patronage, coöperators were driven into the political arena. Plymouth Society, charged with £40,000 of Excess Profits Duty, refused to pay, defeated the Inland Revenue authorities in the courts, and proclaimed this message which the whole Coöperative Movement heard eagerly: "It is because trade unionists are prepared to fight for their rights and to strike for their liberty that they win respect. When the co-operative movement shows equal determination it will receive equal treatment." The late Mr. Bonar Law, who had succeeded Mr. Reginald McKenna as Chancellor, repealed that impost on coöperative societies, confessing that there was "no legal justification for taking Excess Profits Duty where you do not

1. Dean E. A. Burroughs, quoted in A. V. Alexander, *Parliament and the Consumer*, p. 11.

find income tax." An early move of the next Coalition Government was to endeavor, on the basis of a majority recommendation of a Royal Commission, to "find income tax" in the surpluses of mutual trading. It was decreed that "any part of the net proceeds not actually returned to members as 'dividend' or 'discount' should be charged to income tax," and that the "wholesale and productive societies should be treated on exactly the same basis as distributive societies." A new Corporation Profits Tax was made applicable to coöperative societies and operated for twelve months before the Government, being defeated on its own Finance Bill by a majority of two votes, restored immunity to mutuality. An injustice Conservative Parliaments were willing to perpetrate but feared to perpetuate was given legislative sanction in 1933 by a National Government led by Mr. J. Ramsay MacDonald, despite his solemn pledge that he would not continue to be a member of any government taxing coöperative dividends.

These were the circumstances in which the Coöperative party was born and the conditions in which its affiliated membership has grown to five millions. The Coöperative party met a coöperative demand in much the same way that the building of a new factory enables coöperators to produce commodities with which private traders refuse to supply them, or the development of a national coöperative newspaper checks the worst excesses of a hostile Press.

At Swansea Congress in 1917 a resolution, proposed by the Parliamentary Committee, "that the time has now arrived for the co-operative movement to take the necessary steps to secure direct representation in Parliament as the only way of effectively voicing its demands and safeguarding its interests," won a large majority. Six months later, a special national conference approved "a draft scheme for securing co-operative representation in Parliament and on local municipal and administrative bodies" and established a National Coöperative Representation Committee. By January, 1918, the Coöperative Movement, in the person of Mr. Henry J. May (now secretary of the International Coöperative Alliance), had contested its first by-election. In the general ("Khaki") election of 1918, ten candidates ran for office, one being elected. In 1922 eleven coöperative candidates contested seats, four being returned. In 1923, six Coöperative party nominees were elected, one, Mr. A. V. Alexander, being appointed Parliamentary Secretary to the Board of Trade in the first Labor administration. A year later, direct coöperative representation was reduced to five, rose to nine in 1929, when Mr. Alexander became First Lord of the Admiralty, Mr. Alfred Barnes a Lord Commissioner of the Treasury, and Mr. Thomas Henderson Comptroller of the King's Household in the second Labor administration, and fell to one in the 1931 election. There are nine coöperative members in the present Parliament.

As this brief record suggests, the political fortunes of the Coöperative party (founded in 1919 to displace the National Coöperative Representation Committee) have fluctuated with the fortunes of the Labor party with which the British Coöperative Movement, right from the moment of its entry into politics, has been in alliance although not in affiliation. An agreement passed by Cheltenham Congress in 1926 settled "the basis of common working" between the two parties but, as recently as September, 1935, the National Coöperative Authority reaffirmed its desire to retain its political independence. In reply to an invitation to join and become an integral part of the National Council of Labor, which consists of the Labor party, the Parliamentary Labor party and the Trades Union Congress, the Authority stated:

". . . we feel it is not necessary for the co-operative movement to be affiliated to, and become a part of, the National Council of Labour as many of the matters considered by that Council are outside the interests of the co-operative movement as such. We are, however, willing and desirous of having means for consultation with the Executive Committee of the Labour Party on all matters affecting co-operative trade or on subjects in which our movement has especial interest."

What, then, is the structure and policy of the Coöperative party? The party is an offshoot of the Coöperative Union. It holds its own annual conference, representative of its local political councils and branches, and of its own affiliated organizations, like the Women's Coöperative Guild. The policy adopted by conference is submitted for approval to the annual Congress of the Coöperative Union. These local coöperative political councils and branches associate with local Labor parties in joint campaigns and, where the "Cheltenham Agreement" works smoothly, they may nominate municipal and Parliamentary candidates to the local Labor party's selection conference on the same terms as trade unions or other bodies affiliated directly to the Labor party. The national program of the Coöperative party, enunciated in 1922, is crystallized in its opening paragraphs: "(1) To safeguard effectually the interests of voluntary Co-operation, and to resist any legislative or administrative inequality which would hamper its progress, (so) (2) That eventually the processes of production, distribution, and exchange (including the land) shall be organised on co-operative lines in the interests of the whole community."[2]

Obviously, the Coöperative party chants the same political tune as the Labor party. But it orchestrates the theme differently, since practical Coöperation cannot play second fiddle to visionary Socialism. The task of the Coöperative party is twofold: to make the mass of coöperators politically conscious and to permeate the Labor party with knowledge of coöperative ideas and practice.

In its first task, the Coöperative party may be said to have succeeded. Having won the confidence of the trading federations and of retail societies with a large majority of the coöperative membership, it is engaged now in a ceaseless effort

2. T. W. Mercer, *Towards the Coöperative Commonwealth*, p. 179.

to unify the diversified interests of individual consumers into a political policy. The effort is fraught with difficulty. From the days of Rochdale, coöperators have pursued a political ideal—"to arrange the powers of production, distribution, education and government"—but, absorbed in the details of business, they have devoted little attention to formulating political programs. The Christian Socialists protested against an economic system which, since it related human rights to private possession, divided society into warring groups and converted the labor of man "made in God's image" into a commodity bought and sold in the market place. Condemning the scramble for wealth, they pleaded that man's competitive instinct should be removed from the physical to the intellectual plane. For free competition, in which the gain of one is the loss of all, they desired to substitute emulation in Coöperation, in which the gain of each is the gain of all.

Like Robert Owen and Dr. William King (1786–1865), advocate of the Union Shops of 1828, however, the Christian Socialists spoke less in the language of politicians than with the tongues of prophets. As a result, modern coöperators entered politics without any clearly defined political philosophy. They took political action to defend a business rather than to advance a cause, and their political propaganda has been circumscribed by that fact. This restriction, hampering though it may have been to dramatic political progress, has served the public well. In the Right Honorable A. V. Alexander, leader of the Coöperative party in Parliament, the consumer has a spokesman commanding national esteem both as Cabinet Minister and Front Bench Opposition spokesman. Secretary of the Joint-Parliamentary Committee of the Coöperative Congress, Mr. Alexander is witness-in-chief for coöperators before governmental commissions and committees. His grasp of detail and his capacity in debate have established him among the first half dozen politicians in Great Britain. Mr. Alfred Barnes, chairman of the Coöperative party, may be described as the democratic businessman in politics. He, too, occupies a considerable position in political life. Formerly chairman of the London Coöperative Society, his forceful personality was a potent factor in effecting the amalgamation of retail societies which put London Coöperation on the map. Such Members of Parliament have reinforced the Parliamentary efficiency and the public appeal of the Labor party.

The Coöperative Movement is bound to the Labor party by the kinship of common birth and growth and aspiration. The Labor party is the child of Trade Unionism which, like Coöperation, derives from Owenism and is a product of the working-class struggle against poverty. Yet in its second task of permeating Labor with coöperative ideas, the Coöperative party has met with peculiar obstacles despite the valuable contribution made by Coöperation to the romantic rise of Labor in politics.

Between 1906 and 1929, Labor increased its poll from 300,000 to over 8,000,000 votes and almost captured a clear majority of Parliamentary seats—a feat which, accomplished by a process of political education and propaganda, and in face of the fiercest opposition of wealth and privilege, compares favorably with the triumphs of dictators backed by the cash and cannons of vested interests. Organized Labor has inspired developments in municipal trading, initiated expansion of social services, and habituated the minds of men to the idea of peaceful change. There is no exaggeration in the statement that, during the twenty-five years when Labor grew from a movement of protest into a potential government, the intellectual case for Socialism was won in Great Britain. Since then, the party has reeled under a shattering blow. Deserted by its leaders, it failed as a government to ride the economic storm of 1931 and became an easy victim of a combination of the older parties. Yet the heart of Labor, the spirit of its rank and file in the constituencies, remained unbroken. By 1935 the party had regained an electoral position in which complete success was again within grasp, and

Labor, if wisely and courageously led, is a party of brilliant promise.

Supported by trade unionists who, engaged in a hand to hand struggle with capitalists for higher wages, look to nationalization of industry as the fruit of political victory, the Labor party is the political weapon of the working classes. Its historic mission has been to free the working classes from political dependence upon either Conservatives, historic representatives of the landowning class; or Liberals, historic representatives of the factoryowning and financier classes. Labor, clearly, is a class party. But in a democratic State whose social conscience Labor itself has awakened, and in which the rewards of voluntary, collective effort have been considerable, the fact of class struggle is not recognized widely and the waging of a class war is repugnant, even to many of its victims. The Labor party, while denouncing capitalist civilization because of the class divisions it perpetuates, abhors class struggle. It looks to an expansion of social services to redistribute national wealth equitably. It expects an extension of State and municipal trading to bring order out of economic chaos. Its policy is a policy of gradualness, of the slow transformation of industry from individualism to Socialism, on a plan providing for the compensation of the capitalist whom the State would dispossess.

More social services mean additional tax burdens and new overhead charges on privately owned industry. Compensation implies, besides the opening up of alternative fields for private investment, fresh debt burdens on public funds. Labor's plan, therefore, depends for its success on a continuous expansion of wealth production and a continuous drive toward State and municipal enterprise whatever the political complexion of the government in power.

Politically, this prospect has been blurred by the nature of Conservative action during the last ten years. Municipal trading, especially in transport, banking and electricity, far from being encouraged, has been blocked. The State has entered industry, not to expand production, but to restrict output and to stabilize existing forms of organization. Legislation has been directed toward crippling Trade Unionism and placing limitations upon the growth of the Coöperative Movement. Economically, it is open to question whether, in view of the progressive collapse of world and national Capitalism, Labor's plan has not been so endangered as to be out-of-date. There is, for example, the effect upon Great Britain of the upsurge of rival Imperialisms. The black man, and more particularly the yellow man, is ceasing to bear the white man's burdens. Income from colonial exploitation declines and no longer satisfies the demands of rentiers for interest on investments. Thus the toll of profit now presses more heavily upon the worker in the home market. Again, the rapid mobilization of industry into antisocial monopolies subsidized by the State and despoiling consumers is not an accident. It is a symptom of increasing embarrassment of profit-seeking Capitalism; it is a new facet of an old problem. Clinging to its plan, Labor has been obliged to acquiesce in these forms of State activity, and indeed, to initiate some of them, at the expense both of Socialist principle and political expediency.[3] In the era of expanding Capitalism, Labor was a Free Trade party. In the era of declining Capitalism, many sections of Labor advocate Protection. Beyond doubt, Labor's long-term program aims at controlling and directing and, ultimately, superseding capitalist enterprise. It is, however, difficult to escape the conclusion that Labor's immediate policy is conditioned more by capitalist demands than by socialist objectives.

Now, this is not a case against nationalization, which is an essential principle of economic reconstruction. Neither is it the case against compensating owners when dispossessing them of property to which the State, by taxing their property, has given them a good and legitimate title. It is an explanation of Labor's dilemma. Dominated, not improperly, by trade

3. For an outline of Labor's attitude to Protection, see chap. IV.

unionists, Labor finds difficulty in enthusing the consumer, since it would raise the price of his coal to provide miners with higher wages in the process of nationalizing an almost bankrupt industry. Nor does Labor win the growing class of technicians thrown up by changes in industry. It is not improbable that the votes of these technicians now decide the fate of parties at the polls. Although attracted by Labor's idealism and necessary to Labor's electoral and governmental success, they do not identify themselves readily with trade unionists. They are unconcerned about the mere administrative act of nationalization, whether it is encompassed by compensation or confiscation of private property. They are much more concerned to rescue agriculture from its neolithic organization than to dispossess landowners. Capable of visualizing the fruits of the marriage of science and natural resources, their cry is for opportunity to *create*. While Labor wrangles about the method of nationalizing industries, and invites the criticism that it would give some private owners fixed rewards in perpetuity in return for industries that are wasting assets, the "united front" of artisans and technicians remains a dream, and the leading intellectuals, who ten years ago were among Labor's strongest allies, either eschew politics, or, chafing at the slowness of economic change, envisage a speedy overthrow of Capitalism by the forces of the extreme Left.

In short, many consumers and technicians argue that modern conditions require a reorientation of Labor policy. They insist that the State should take over, not this industry or that, but the banks which are the source of credit, and the land, which absorbs every increment of communal enterprise. Thus wages and rewards would become at once a question of social policy unrelated to the economic position of individual industries. Thereafter, the State would foster and own new industries, leaving the old to be competed out of business, or reorganized or nationalized in conformity with a plan designed to increase all wealth production. To the question,

"What shall we do with the capitalist?" the modern technician returns, in effect, the answer given by the Pioneers of Rochdale ninety-three years ago: "We shall coöperate and do without him."

Whatever the merits of this policy, its conception of the consumer commanding a place in society is as hard for the trade unionist to grasp as for the capitalist to concede. Trade unionists, of course, are animated by social ideals. They have given powerful lip service to Coöperation and, in Parliament, have been consistent defenders of the consumer. But trade unionism in action has shown little regard hitherto either for the consumer or the Coöperative Movement. In the General Strike of 1926, to take one instance, dairymen and bakers were called out in common with other types of labor. Apart from the irritation thus caused to the whole community and the danger that a food shortage would undermine the morale of the strikers themselves, the fact that the only dairymen and bakers then organized in trade unions were employees of coöperative societies was overlooked. While coöperative societies were advancing credit to strikers, coöperative bread and milk business was being deflected to trade rivals employing nonunion labor!

How important is this question of approach to economic problems and why the Coöperative Movement values so highly its political independence are revealed in the reorganization of British agriculture since 1931.

Coöperators advocate joint control of all marketing schemes by producers, distributors and consumers. They envisage a complete coöperative service from producer to consumer. On the evidence of the legislative activity of the second Labor Government, Labor accepts producer organization as the preliminary to a national organization of manufacture and distribution, and regards the introduction of a balancing element of consumer control as a later development. "The two policies," the National Coöperative Authority told Congress in 1936, "whilst being designed for similar ends, involved very different conceptions as to the control of imports and the desirability of municipal expansion in trading. On the one hand, the co-operative movement contended that co-operative permeation of the whole marketing structure was the desirable line of approach towards State control; whilst the Labor Party felt that national control was the main issue and that within such control the co-operative movement would receive every encouragement." Both sides are striving sincerely to bridge a gulf the width of which may be said, quite fairly, to measure Labor's unawareness of the achievements and potentialities of Coöperation. Labor's Agricultural Marketing Act of 1931, on which succeeding governments have found it easy to graft quota schemes and licensing regulations, has encouraged the creation of giant monopolies and contributed little to the improvement of agricultural economy. The facts are now realized. Thus the tendency of present collaboration is toward providing coöperators with facilities to bring essential commodities under public control through effective competition with capitalist agencies—an evolutionary development, in the words of the National Coöperative Authority, "now regarded as far more practical than a spectacular overthrow of Capitalism by statutory means"; and, it may be added, a clear departure from Labor's former nationalization-cum-compensation policy and an indication of a more realistic approach to the problems of peaceful economic change.

Loyalty to the Labor party in the exceptional difficulties it has encountered recently may have prevented the Coöperative party from criticizing more sharply trends in Labor's policy which, besides being at variance with consumer interests, would be hard to justify from the viewpoint of social progress. It may be anticipated that, as the two movements become more integrated, the influence of Coöperation upon Labor's program will become more marked. The Left is proud of coöperative achievement. It points to business democracy in control of a trade and finance turnover exceeding

£1,000,000,000 a year as proof of Labor's fitness to govern. Yet it still ignores Coöperation's day-to-day experience and the possibility that in Coöperation there is a living, growing alternative to Capitalism; and the further Left one looks the more ignorant men seem to be of the value of the weapons within their grasp. What Labor must learn is that a Movement engaged in social distribution offers one medium through which some measure of social production may be achieved. Advance to social production is a requisite of the revitalized democracy upon which reformers set their hopes.

Measured statistically, the standard of living over long periods remains constant. Measured realistically—in terms of what people expect from life, the intensification of productive processes, and what, in the way of food, fuel, shelter and the amenities of civilization, Capitalism now offers them—the standard of living falls steadily. Unemployment fluctuates, but at ever higher levels. Its victims, once a minority of unemployables, are now a substantial proportion of the whole working class and include highly skilled men and women for whom Capitalism has ceased to have any use. One tenth of the population, in spite of the relief afforded them from public funds, lives in a state of semistarvation. One half of the population does not get enough of the right kind of food to eat. That food consumption depends upon income is no longer an argument advanced by sentimentalists. It is a truth established by an overwhelming volume of independent expert opinion whose influence the official denial of governments and their newspapers has been unable to counteract. Harsh social facts, like the decline in the birth rate, point to a profound discouragement with existing society and threaten family life and the stability of the social structure. In every political party there is a demand for social investigation amounting to a passion similar to that which swept all people of good will forty years ago, and the revelation of the abysmal poverty to which the larger section of the community is condemned forces, even upon reluctant governments, new legislation regulating the conditions and rewards of labor. Regulation, however, cannot purge economic anarchy of its evils. The limits to which capitalist industry can be bolstered by the imposition of tariffs and the stimulations of monopolies are already within sight. Economically, Great Britain is a Corporate State, differing from the Continental model only in this one particular: that the burden of sustaining industries fostered by Government falls more directly on the masses as consumers than upon producers in fields, factories, and workshops.

The nation's social conscience is not dead. Englishmen enjoy a heritage of personal freedom and of public service that is dear to them. The voices of violence, whatever brand of dictatorship they preach, are few. The first blast on the trumpets of anti-Semitism merely filled decent citizens with disgust. Politically, Fascism has no roots in Great Britain. It is true that, under the strains and stresses of economic decay, all England long since ceased to be Liberal. But all England, from the more vital elements in the Conservative party on the Right to the more responsible elements of the Communist party on the Left, is democratic.

Yet desire to avoid the clash of class does not resolve the facts of class. The race is between economic collapse, the unknown horrors collapse would unleash, and the rise of a united democratic movement with a practical program of far-reaching social change and the will to make its program effective against the vested interests now rallying in defense of their privilege. The side on which the Coöperative Movement will stand in that struggle is not in doubt. The value of its strength and example will depend upon the vigor and courage of its political representatives and upon the wisdom shown by organized Labor in learning the lesson Coöperation has to teach.

XIV.

Prospectus

WHAT do coöperators create?" Sir Frederick Marquis, leading chain store magnate, asked rhetorically during a debate in which the case for Coöperation was broadcast to the people of Great Britain for the first time.[1] The rhetorical answer is that coöperators are creating an alternative to the muddle of private trade. That alternative is so satisfying to consumers that more and more of them are intrusting Coöperation with their trade and savings, and consumers are deriving from Coöperation such social and economic benefits that neither the pressure of trusts nor the attacks of politicians can stay its growth. Thus the prospects of Coöperation are bounded only by the Movement's own vision and enterprise.

On the basis of the known market, Coöperation is freeing price from profit, emancipating enterprise from speculation, enriching consumers and thereby increasing the demand for labor. The success of the Ten-Year Plan will hasten this process and may well make the Coöperative Movement the most stabilizing factor, in terms of prices and employment, in the capitalist State.

Coöperative trade in Great Britain, however, is largely a one-way trade. Through Coöperation, citizens organize themselves as consumers to supply their wants. Goods and services flow *to them* in an overwhelmingly greater volume than *from them* to other people. For coöperators there is still an empire of production to be conquered, an empire as wide as the world itself. That consumers can coöperate for the sale of their own products has been proven by experience. Spurred on by boycott, they have turned to the production of hun-

1. British Broadcasting Corporation, February 9, 1937.

dreds of commodities formerly outside their control. To the factory, the farm and the coal mine they have brought the boon of their scientifically measured demand and the economies of coöperative insurance and banking. Coöperative productive enterprise has been concentrated mainly upon secondary commodities like shoes and soap and shirts. The field of primary production awaits the coming of Coöperation to rescue it from the fever of boom and the slough of slump.

Ten years ago hopes were high that an International Coöperative Wholesale Society, then springing into active life under the inspiration of the International Coöperative Alliance[2] would canalize the export operations of national coöperative movements and proceed, in due course, to carry Coöperation into international trade. Fascism and Nazism on the continent of Europe, and the sudden enthusiasm evinced by capitalist States for economic nationalism and self-immolation have since 1931 frustrated, although they have failed to kill, these hopes. The regulation of imports by State license has been especially inimical to world-wide Coöperation. Taking a given year as basic—usually a year prior to the introduction of control—national governments have granted importers licenses to the value of their imports during the basic year. In consequence, coöperative federations opening up new departments after the basic year have found it difficult or impossible to obtain licenses for the import of goods essential to their new enterprises. Thus private businesses have been endowed by statute with an impenetrable monopoly. In 1935 the members of the International C.W.S. imported goods to the value of £44,000,000, the British share being £34,000,000 and one quarter of the total being American in its origin. The bulk of these imports was effected through private channels. Exports totaled £1,650,000, of

2. The International Coöperative Alliance is a federation of coöperative organizations throughout the world. At present it includes 143 federations with 100,000,000 members in 40 countries.

which nearly £1,000,000 went direct to coöperative organizations. Most of this trade was in food and raw materials. In an endeavor to defeat legislative restrictions, some national coöperative organizations, notably the C.W.S., the Scottish C.W.S. and the Scandinavian Movement, have established buying agencies overseas. The results have been of some economic significance. C.W.S. imports of foodstuffs, or primary products, from New Zealand, for example, have been paid for by C.W.S. exports of manufactured goods or secondary products to New Zealand. This exchange of foods for goods has not followed any loan; the C.W.S. has no capital invested in New Zealand. It has not followed any flag; the C.W.S. has no Imperialist interests. It is a natural trade arising from the natural desire of two sections of the world community to satisfy their natural wants. It is barter. It is Free Trade in a sense unknown to competitive Capitalism or the London money market which, conceiving Free Trade to be the exchange of goods for debts, resorted to Protection when interest on overseas investment began to decline and sought to make good at the expense of home consumers the fall in their earnings from the exploitation of foreign labor. It is Free Trade in accord with common sense and in conformity with the ideal of free Coöperation.

Not less significant have been International C.W.S. experiments in joint purchasing of dried fruits from America and the Near East. In 1935 these joint purchases from America trebled in volume. They point to the possibility of national coöperative organizations throughout the world pooling their markets for, say, oil supplies from American coöperative refiners. The logical development of such a step might be the acquiring of oil wells by a federation of national coöperative societies, and an effective attempt to break the monopoly power of the international oil trusts. Upon the British Movement, with its unrivaled resources and great administrative experience, rests much of the responsibility for converting coöperative trade into a two-way traffic and carrying the Pioneers' conception of consumers' Coöperation to completion.

Assuming the return of a Labor Government, the economic climate at home may change, may become more favorable to Coöperation. Coöperators will ask nothing more than the breaking of the shackles, legal, economic and fiscal, clamped upon their movements by frightened private traders. Under equal conditions, their demonstrable superiority would enable them to expand enormously the nonspeculative market in which they operate. Expanding their known market, they would also increase their surpluses and release new resources for improving the quality and design of goods and eliminating the mass of the cheap and shoddy which, today, renders so much of the spending of the nation's income wasteful and uneconomic. The effect upon all forms of production and distribution would be salutary. The profit motive would become secondary to service over an increasing area of commerce. Willingness to socialize enterprise would become a requisite of business survival.

This is one way, and a traditional British way, to that peaceful economic change which the cause of democracy and the needs of the times so urgently demand.

Appendix

Coöperative Products of the Coöperative Wholesale Society

Aerated Waters
Aluminiumware
Bacon and Hams
Bedding
Bedsteads—iron, brass and wood
Biscuits
Blankets
Bluing—square, round and oval
Boots and shoes
Brushes and brooms
Building
Butter
Cakes
Calico
Candied Peel
Candles—paraffin, stearine, and tallow
Canned foods
Caps
Cardboard boxes
Cardigans
Cheese
Chemicals
Chocolate confectionery
Cloth and clothing, ready-made or to measure
Coal
Coal wagons
Cocoa
Coffee, pure and blended
Colored cotton goods
Condensed milk
Confectionery
Corsets
Crockery
Cutlery
Cycles and motor cycles
Drugs, etc.,
Dyes
Earthenware jars
Electrical appliances
Emulsion—cod liver oil
Enamelware
Engineering
Feeding cakes and meals
Fenders and curbs
Fire irons and brasses
Flannels
Flour
Fruits, in bottles and tins
Furniture—suites, dressers, sideboards, etc.
Fustians, corduroys, etc.
Galvanized ware
Glass bottles and jars
Gloves
Glue
Glycerine
Hardware—buckets, baths, etc.
Hats and caps
Hosiery and knitted underwear
Household utensils

Infants' food

Jackets, in bluette, duck, etc.

Jams—pure sugar and fresh fruit

Jellies

Jerseys

Jewelry

Lard

Leather

Leather bags

Linings

Mantles, including ladies' costumes, jackets, etc.

Margarine

Marmalade

Mats

Mattresses—wire, wool, flock, or hair

Medicines

Milk (bottled, condensed and dried)

Millinery

Mincemeat

Night lights

Oat cakes

Oil cakes

Oils

Overalls, cord drawers, etc.

Packing boxes

Paints, varnishes, enamels and distempers

Pants

Pepper

Pickles

Picture frames

Pinafores and blouses

Polish, for boots, etc., metal polish

Portmanteaux

Potted meats

Prams and folding cars

Preserves

Printing, bookbinding and lithography in all branches

Quilts, down and wadded

Rope and twine

Rugs

Saddlery

Sauces

Scales and weighing machines

Sheetings

Shirtings and grandrill

Shirts

Shop fittings

Silesias (window shades)

Size

Soaps

Starch—white, blue and cream

Suet (Sutox)

Sweets, boiled, also gums, jellies, pastilles, etc.

Tea

Tinware—flour bins, traveling trunks, etc.

Tobacco, cigars, cigarettes, and snuff

Umbrellas

Underclothing

Varnishes

Vinegar

Washing, wringing, mangling and weighing machines, etc.

Wheelwrighting

Wireless

Woolens

Yeast

Bibliography

THE reader who desires to study further the subject of Co-operation will find valuable information in the following books and pamphlets:

FLANAGAN, J. A. Wholesale coöperation in Scotland.
HALL, F. Handbook for members of coöperative committees.
HALL, F. *and* WATKINS, W. P. Coöperation.
HAYWARD, SIR FRED. The coöperative boycott.
MERCER, T. W. Dr. William King the coöperator (1828–30).
PALMER, R. A. Legal limitations on coöperative progress.
RUSSELL, GEORGE ("Æ"). The national being.
TOMLINSON, CHARLES E. A survey of coöperative production.
TWIGG, H. J. The economic advance of British coöperation (annually).
WEBB, CATHERINE. The woman with the basket.
WEBB, SIDNEY *and* BEATRICE. The consumers' coöperative movement.

Addenda and Errata

p. 20, line 17. *For* Kensington *read* Kennington.

p. 29, line 11. *Read* the time in getting goods.

p. 35, line 4. *For* 1884 *read* 1889.

p. 44, line 10. *For* £7,000,000,000 *read* £8,700,000,000.

p. 44, line 18. *For* shopping *read* shipping.

p. 48, line 15. *For* £7,000 *read* £5,000.

p. 48, line 19. *For* £5,000 *read* £3,000.

p. 48, line 21. *For* £5,000 *read* £3,000.

p. 57, line 19. *For* .05 per cent *read* .02.

p. 58, line 3. ⎫
p. 145, line 7. ⎬ *For* Company Acts *read* Companies Acts.
p. 149, line 29. ⎭

p. 61, line 11. *For* tiny *read* nine.

p. 61, line 12. *For* Stornaway *read* Stornoway.

p. 89, line 33, to p. 90, line 5. As this book goes to press the House of Lords is engaged in a case which may end the paradox.

p. 92, line 27. *Read* could not be credited.

p. 99, line 30. *For* 80,000,000 *read* 130,000,000.

p. 101, line 11. *For* £1,400,000,000 *read* £1,350,000,000.

p. 101, line 12. *For* £1,085,000 *read* £1,089,000,000.

p. 102, lines 16–17. *For* 4,750,000,000 *read* 4,750,000.

p. 114, line 6. *Read* because concentration of capital.

p. 117, line 12. *For* 4s.8d. *read* 1s.9d.

p. 135, lines 11–20. This was possible until 1937 when County Court rules were applied.

p. 137, footnote 6. *For* Walker *read* Walter.

p. 167, footnote. *For* type face *read* coat-of-arms.

p. 170, footnote 6. *Read* Evidence before Departmental Committee on the Companies Acts, 1908–17. *Financial Democracy*, p. 81.

p. 180, line 14. *For* two *read* three.

Index